Exploring Key Issues in Early Childhood and Technology

Exploring Key Issues in Early Childhood and Technology offers early childhood allies, both in the classroom and out, a cutting-edge overview of the most important topics related to technology and media use in the early years.

In this powerful resource, international experts share their wealth of experience and unpack complex issues into a collection of accessibly written essays. This text is specifically geared towards practitioners looking for actionable information on screen time, cybersafety, makerspaces, coding, computational thinking, STEM, AI and other core issues related to technology and young children in educational settings. Influential thought leaders draw on their own experiences and perspectives, addressing the big ideas, opportunities and challenges around the use of technology and digital media in early childhood. Each chapter provides applications and inspiration, concluding with essential lessons learned, actionable next steps and a helpful list of recommended further reading and resources.

This book is a must-read for anyone looking to explore what we know – and what we still need to know – about the intersection between young children, technology and media in the digital age.

Chip Donohue, Ph.D., is Founding Director of the Technology in Early Childhood (TEC) Center at Erikson Institute, where he served as Dean of Distance Learning and Continuing Education between 2009 and 2018. He is a Senior Fellow and Advisor of the Fred Rogers Center for Early Learning and Children's Media at Saint Vincent College.

Exploring Key Issues in Early Childhood and Technology

Evolving Perspectives and Innovative Approaches

Edited by Chip Donohue

Routledge
Taylor & Francis Group

NEW YORK AND LONDON

First published 2020
by Routledge
52 Vanderbilt Avenue, New York, NY 10017

and by Routledge
2 Park Square, Milton Park, Abingdon, Oxon, OX14 4RN

Routledge is an imprint of the Taylor & Francis Group, an informa business

© 2020 Taylor & Francis

The right of Chip Donohue to be identified as the author of the editorial material, and of the authors for their individual chapters, has been asserted in accordance with sections 77 and 78 of the Copyright, Designs and Patents Act 1988.

Trademark notice: Product or corporate names may be trademarks or registered trademarks, and are used only for identification and explanation without intent to infringe.

Library of Congress Cataloging in Publication Data
Names: Donohue, Chip, editor.
Title: Exploring key issues in early childhood and technology : evolving perspectives and innovative approaches / edited by Chip Donohue.
Description: New York, NY : Routledge, 2020. |
Includes bibliographical references and index.
Identifiers: LCCN 2019009235 (print) | LCCN 2019013387 (ebook)
| ISBN 9780429457425 (eBook) | ISBN 9781138313798 (hardback)
| ISBN 9781138313804 (pbk.)
Subjects: LCSH: Early childhood education–Computer-assisted instruction. | Educational technology. | Computers and children.
Classification: LCC LB1139.35.C64 (ebook) | LCC LB1139.35.C64 E96 2020 (print) | DDC 372.21–dc23
LC record available at https://lccn.loc.gov/2019009235

ISBN: 978-1-138-31379-8 (hbk)
ISBN: 978-1-138-31380-4 (pbk)
ISBN: 978-0-429-45742-5 (ebk)

Typeset in Bembo
by Swales & Willis, Exeter, Devon, UK

Printed in Canada

This book is a collection of essays about young children and technology written by thought leaders and innovators in child development, early childhood education, teacher education, research, children's media, public media, pediatrics and public policy. The contributing authors have reflected on their work and what they have learned and shared their visions of where we need to go to best support young children, families and educators in the digital age.

On behalf of these thought leaders who have contributed to this collection, I dedicate this book and our collective efforts to the early childhood educators in classrooms, home-based programs and informal learning environments beyond the classroom who are translating research and key issues into practice and pioneering innovative approaches every day. In the process of integrating technology in appropriate and intentional ways, they have developed their own perspectives, articulated big ideas and become influential thought leaders in their own right. And we acknowledge the essential roles played by all the other grown-ups in children's lives – everyone who is engaged in parenting a child or works with or on behalf of young children and families. In embracing the role of media mentor, they engage and empower young children to safely navigate the always changing world of screens, media, social media and emerging technologies.

In the pages that follow we'll share powerful ideas about young children and technology. You'll learn about our evolving perspectives and the innovative approaches we each champion. And while we're excited to share our thoughts with you, we want you to know that we stand in awe of the powerful ideas you bring to your work and relationships with children and families every day.

Contents

Afterword   **120**
CHIP DONOHUE

Contributors

Chip Donohue, PhD, is Founding Director of the Technology in Early Childhood (TEC) Center at Erikson Institute in Chicago where he was the Dean of Distance Learning and Continuing Education from 2009 to 2018. He is a Senior Fellow and Member of the Advisory Board of the Fred Rogers Center for Early Learning and Children's Media at Saint Vincent College, where he and Roberta Schomburg co-chaired the working group that developed the 2012 NAEYC (National Association for the Education of Young Children) and Fred Rogers Center Joint Position Statement on *Technology and Interactive Media as Tools in Early Childhood Programs Serving Children from Birth through Age 8*. In addition to this book, *Exploring Key Issues in Early Childhood and Technology: Evolving Perspectives and Innovative Approaches*, Chip is the editor of two previous books, *Family Engagement in the Digital Age: Early Childhood Educators as Media Mentors* (2017), and *Technology and Digital Media in the Early Years: Tools for Teaching and Learning* (2015), both co-published by Routledge/NAEYC. He is also co-editor, with Susan Friedman and Tamara Kaldor, of an upcoming NAEYC publication, *The Essentials: Developmentally Appropriate Technology Practice in the Classroom* (2019). In 2012 he received the Bammy Award and Educators' Voice Award as *Innovator of the Year* from the Academy of Education Arts and Sciences. In 2015, he was honored as a children's media *Emerging Pioneer* at the KAPi (Kids At Play International) Awards.

Meet the Thought Leaders

Lewis J. Bernstein, PhD, is the President of Lewis J. Bernstein and Associates, a company he founded after retiring as Executive Vice President of Education and Research at Sesame Workshop. Dr. Bernstein's association with *Sesame Street* began in 1972, when he came on board as Director of Research, working alongside the creative geniuses Joan Ganz Cooney, Jim Henson and Jon Stone, to integrate education into the entertainment aspect of children's television. His 40-plus-year career at Sesame Workshop was defined by his passion to improve the intellectual, social, emotional and moral lives of children through media, both as an educator and as a producer. As Executive VP, Education, Research and Outreach, Dr. Bernstein's responsibilities included establishing the overall educational agenda – direction and content – for all of Sesame Workshop's domestic and international programs, reaching millions of children all over the world – regardless of economic status, gender, religion, or culture. In his creative capacities at the Workshop, Dr. Bernstein served as Executive Producer of domestic *Sesame Street, Rechov Sumsum/Shara'a Simsim* (an Israeli–Palestinian co-production of *Sesame Street*) and the *Shalom Sesame* and *Sesame English* series. Together with associates in his company, Lewis J. Bernstein and Associates, LLC, he is currently using his expertise and experience advising major foundations, corporations and platforms, on the creation of youth-oriented programs to educate, inspire and empower youth to work on improving themselves and the world they are inheriting.

Marina Umaschi Bers, PhD, is a professor at the Eliot-Pearson Department of Child Study and Human Development and an adjunct professor in the Computer Science Department at Tufts University, where she heads the interdisciplinary Developmental Technologies (DevTech) Research Group. Her research involves the design and study of innovative learning technologies to promote children's positive development, most specifically in early childhood. She co-designed the free ScratchJr programming language, which has over 11.5 million downloads, and she developed the KIBO robot kit for children 4 to 7 years old, that can be programmed with wooden blocks without using keyboards or screens and is currently used in over 54 countries. Dr. Bers' theoretical approach, as well as the curriculum and assessment methods she developed, can be found in her books, *Coding as Playground: Programming and Computational Thinking in the Early Childhood Classroom* (Routledge, 2018); *The Official ScratchJr Book* (No Starch Press, 2015); *Designing Digital Experiences for Positive Youth Development: From Playpen to Playground* (Oxford University Press, 2012); and *Blocks to Robots: Learning with Technology in the Early Childhood Classroom* (Teachers College Press, 2008). Dr. Bers received an MEd from Boston University and an MS and PhD from the MIT Media Laboratory working with Seymour Papert.

Warren Buckleitner, PhD, is an educational researcher and product reviewer with a specialty in the design of interactive media. He is a Senior Fellow of the Fred Rogers Center for Early Learning and Children's Media at Saint Vincent College, an Assistant Professor and teaches interactive design at The College of New Jersey and is the Editor of *Children's Technology Review*. He covered children's technology for *The New York Times* for over a decade. In 2001 he created the Dust or Magic Institute, an annual meeting of leading designers, researchers and reviewers, with the intention to share examples of best practice in digital media. That same year, he started Mediatech Foundation, a non-profit technology center designed to enhance the services of a small-town public library with technology. He's the coordinator of the annual BolognaRagazzi Digital Award and the KAPi Awards – a juried prize given each year at the Consumer Electronics Show (CES). He has taught in NYU's ITP program, Rutgers GSE and Michigan State University. He holds a BS in Elementary Education (*cum laude*), an MS in Human Development and a doctorate in educational psychology (Learning, Technology & Culture) from Michigan State University. He is married with two daughters, is a new grandfather and enjoys playing the trumpet.

Milton Chen, PhD, is Senior Fellow at the George Lucas Educational Foundation (GLEF) in the Bay Area, which produces the award-winning edutopia.org website on innovative K-12 learning. He served as executive director of GLEF from 1998 to 2010. Dr. Chen has been the founding director of the KQED Center for Education in San Francisco; director of research at Sesame Workshop in New York, helping develop *Sesame Street, The Electric Company* and *3-2-1 Contact*; and has been an assistant professor at the Harvard Graduate School of Education. During 2007 to 2008, he was one of 35 Fulbright New Century Scholars. Dr. Chen serves as chairman of the Panasonic Foundation, which supports STEM learning in Newark, NJ, is a member of the board of trustees of the W.K. Kellogg Foundation (WKKF) and is on the board of trustees for Sesame Workshop. He chaired the education committee for the National Park System Advisory Board, advancing youth learning in STEM and US history. Dr. Chen's career has been honored by the Fred Rogers Award from the Corporation for Public Broadcasting and the Congressional Black Caucus. He has received the NHK–Japan President's Award for contributions to educational media and was named an Honorary Ranger by the National Park Service. His 2010 book, *Education Nation: Six Leading Edges of Innovation in our Schools*, was named as one of the year's best education books by the *American School Board Journal*.

Kevin A. Clark is a Professor of Learning Technologies and the Founding Director of the Center for Digital Media Innovation and Diversity at George Mason University. Prior to becoming a professor, Dr. Clark was part of an educational technology startup company, where he managed the design and development of children's educational content for the Sony PlayStation. His research focuses on the role of interactive and digital media in education, broadening participation in STEM and issues of diversity in children's media. His research has been funded by the National Science Foundation (NSF), the Bill & Melinda Gates Foundation, Microsoft, Dell and the Entertainment Software Association (ESA) Foundation. Dr. Clark has extensive experience as a children's media advisor and/or consultant for organizations including the Public Broadcasting Service (PBS), the Corporation for Public Broadcasting (CPB), Cartoon Network, The Jim Henson Company, The Fred Rogers Company, DHX Media, Disney Junior, Toca Boca, Hasbro, Mattel, Facebook, Netflix, Amazon Studios, and WGBH Kids. Dr. Clark is currently a member of the board of directors for Fred Rogers Productions and a member of the Barbie Global Advisory Council. Kevin holds both a BS and an MS in computer science from North Carolina State University and a PhD in Instructional Systems from Pennsylvania State University.

Susan Edwards is Director of the Early Childhood Futures research program in the Institute for Learning Sciences and Teacher Education (ILSTE) at the Australian Catholic University. Her group investigates the role of play-based learning in the early childhood curriculum for the 21st century. Professor Edwards has completed work as a Chief Investigator on two Australian Research Council Discovery Grants: The first examining play-based learning in early childhood education settings; and the second, the role of play-based learning in well-being and sustainability education. She is currently the lead Chief Investigator on an Australian Research Council Discovery Grant on digital play and an Australian Research Council Linkage Project investigating best practice for playgroups-in-schools. Susan has over 70 publications in peer-reviewed journals and has published several books with publishers including Cambridge University Press, Palgrave Macmillan and Open University Press. Her most recent book is *Young Children's Play and Learning in the Digital Age* (co-authored with Christine Stephen, University of Stirling). Professor Edwards co-chaired the Early Childhood Australia (ECA) Digital Policy Group (with Professor Leon Straker), leading the writing of the ECA Statement on Young Children and Digital Technology. Professor Edwards is also a winner of several awards for teaching excellence in the tertiary education sector, including a prestigious Australian Learning and Teaching Council award in 2009.

Shuli Gilutz, PhD, specializes in user experience (UX) research, assessment and strategy of interactive environments for children. She works both in industry and academia, teaching, advising and conducting research, in a variety of user experience settings, as well as as a strategic consultant for development and design of children's digital experiences. Shuli founded the Child-Computer Interaction research group on Facebook, with over 1,000 members worldwide, and works to combine research and practice with startups both at Google Launchpad in Tel-Aviv and MindCET educational technology accelerators. She is a teaching fellow at Tel-Aviv University, as well as part of Shenkar's School of Design Toy Inventor program. She is a global conference speaker about children and digital media, as well as age-appropriate UX, from usability, to play and learning.

Shuli is a board member and research advocate of the Designing for Children's Rights Association, which is an international group partnering with UNICEF to promote ethics and child-centered design.

Lisa Guernsey is director of the Learning Technologies Project and senior advisor to the Early & Elementary Education Policy program at New America. She leads teams of writers and analysts to tell stories, translate research, examine policies and generate ideas for new approaches to education that recognize the implications of new technologies, all aimed at ensuring that historically underserved students and families can thrive. Prior to her work at New America, Guernsey worked as a staff writer at *The New York Times* and *The Chronicle of Higher Education* and has contributed to several other national publications, including *The Atlantic, The Washington Post, Newsweek, Time, Slate* and *USA Today.* She is co-author with Michael H. Levine of *Tap, Click, Read: Growing Readers in a World of Screens* (Jossey-Bass, 2015) and author of *Screen Time: How Electronic Media – From Baby Videos to Educational Software – Affects Your Young Child* (Basic Books, 2012). She won a 2012 Gold Eddie magazine award for a *School Library Journal* article on e-books and has served on several national advisory committees on early education, including the Institute of Medicine's Committee on the Science of Children Birth to Age 8. Guernsey holds a master's in English/American studies and a bachelor's degree in English from the University of Virginia. Lisa lives in Alexandria, Virginia with her two daughters.

David Kleeman is a strategist, analyst, author, speaker and connector. He has led the children's media industry in developing sustainable, child-friendly practices for more than 30 years. He began this work as president of the American Center for Children and Media and is now Senior Vice President of Global Trends for Dubit, a strategy/research consultancy and digital studio. When he began this work, "children's media" meant television. Today, he is fascinated by, and passionate about, children's wide range of possibilities for entertainment, engagement, play and learning. David uses research, insights and experience to show that much may change, but children's developmental path and needs remain constant. David is advisory board chair to the international children's television festival PRIX JEUNESSE, Board Vice President for the National Association for Media Literacy Education (NAMLE) and on the board of the Children's Media Association (CMA) and the Advisory Board of the Joan Ganz Cooney Center. He was a Senior Fellow of the Fred Rogers Center for Early Learning and Children's Media at Saint Vincent College. He travels worldwide seeking best practices in children's entertainment and learning. He has spoken (and, more important, listened!) on six continents and writes extensively for varied audiences.

Natalia Kucirkova is Professorof Early Childhood Education and Development at the University of Stavanger, Norway. Her research concerns innovative ways of supporting children's book reading, digital literacy and exploring the role of personalization in early years. She co-edits the Bloomsbury Book Series *Children's Reading and Writing on Screen* and the journal *Literacy*, published by Wiley. Natalia's research takes place collaboratively across academia, and commercial and third sectors.

Michael H. Levine, a child development, early learning and social policy expert is Chief Knowledge Officer of Sesame Workshop, the global non-profit media organization devoted to promoting the education and healthy development of children. As Chief Knowledge Officer, Dr. Levine is a member of the senior executive team and responsible for driving organization-wide learning, educational partnerships, knowledge exchange and policy leadership. Levine is also the Founding Executive Director of the Joan Ganz Cooney Center, a pioneering thought leader in the digital media and learning field. Previously, Levine was Vice President for the Asia Society, managing interactive media and educational initiatives to promote knowledge and understanding of other world regions, languages and cultures. He conceived and directed a national campaign, *I am Your Child*, with entertainment, policy, philanthropic and practice leaders, which led to major state and national investments in health care, early learning and parenting education. He also previously oversaw Carnegie Corporation's groundbreaking work in early childhood development and educational media. He has authored numerous academic articles, writes for media outlets such as *Slate, Huffington Post* and *Education Week,* and is a frequent keynote speaker at education and technology conferences around the world. His recent book, co-authored with Lisa Guernsey of New America, is *Tap, Click, Read: Growing Readers in a World of Screens* (Jossey-Bass, 2015).

Sonia Livingstone, OBE, is Professor of Social Psychology in the Department of Media and Communications at London School of Economics (LSE). Taking a comparative, critical and contextualized approach, her research examines how the changing conditions of mediation are reshaping everyday practices and possibilities for action. She has published 20 books, with a particular focus on online opportunities and risks for children and young people, media literacy, regulation and children's rights in the digital age. Her most recent book, with Julian Sefton-Green, is *The Class: Living and Learning in the Digital Age* (NYUP, 2016). Sonia was awarded the title of Officer of the Order of the British Empire (OBE) in 2014 "for services to children and child internet safety." Sonia is currently leading the Global Kids Online project (with the UNICEF Office of Research-Innocenti and EU Kids Online), Children's Data and Privacy Online (funded by the Information Commissioner's Office) and co-directing The Nurture

Network. She is also writing a book with Alicia Blum-Ross called *Parenting for a Digital Future* (Oxford University Press) and participates in the European Commission-funded research networks, DigiLitEY and MakEY. She runs a blog called *Parenting for a Digital Future* and contributes to the LSE's *Media Policy Project* blog.

M. Elena Lopez, PhD, is a Co-director at Global Family Research Project (GFRP). She is passionate about applying her research on the connections among families, schools and communities to improve children's learning. Elena has used her research and publications to inform major initiatives, including the Office of Head Start's National Center on Parent, Family and Community Engagement, United Way's Worldwide Family Engagement for High School Success and the Public Library Association's new directions in family engagement in children's learning. She has conceptualized frameworks for teacher training and professional learning and co-edited *Preparing Educators for Family Engagement*, a book of cases based on ecological theory. At the National Center on Parent, Family and Community Engagement she was responsible for initiating digital simulations as a tool for professional learning and reflective supervision. Her professional experiences include evaluating public and philanthropic initiatives to promote children's well-being, managing education and health grants for a philanthropic foundation, and serving on national advisory and governing boards. She received her doctorate in Social Anthropology from Harvard University. She is proud to have two entrepreneurial adult children who are in the education field.

Jackie Marsh is Professor of Education at the University of Sheffield, UK. She is a Fellow of the Academy of Social Sciences and a Fellow of the Royal Society of Arts. Jackie has led numerous research projects engaging children, teachers, parents and children's media industry partners in research on young children's play and digital literacy practices in homes and schools including the ESRC-funded project Technology and Play. Jackie is Chair of COST Action IS1410, DigiLitEY, a European network of 35 countries focusing on research in this area (2015–2019). She is currently leading a seven-country project on makerspaces in the early years, MakEY (2017–2019) funded by the EU Horizon 2020 programme. Jackie has published widely in the field and is a co-editor of the *Journal of Early Childhood Literacy*.

Lydia Plowman is Chair in Education and Technology at the Moray House School of Education, University of Edinburgh and a Fellow of the Academy of Social Sciences. She is internationally recognized for her research on children's play and learning with technology in a range of formal and informal settings and has been actively involved in research, consultancy and knowledge exchange with the children's digital media industry, the BBC, Save the Children, the Children's Media Foundation, the National

Health Service in Scotland, the European Commission and UK and Scottish governments. Lydia has been involved in research about young children's playing and learning with digital media at home and in educational settings for many years and has extensive experience of working with children, family members and educators in ways that enable us to gain insights into their practices, values and attitudes. Current research interests include digital play, the ways in which technology is integrated into family life and the home and observing the interactions of young children and their caregivers with digital media. Recent research investigated the roles of toys, technology and play in the everyday lives of young children at home, building on her initial studies of children's play and learning with technology in preschool and schools.

Jenny Radesky is an Assistant Professor of Developmental Behavioral Pediatrics at the University of Michigan Medical School. She received her MD from Harvard Medical School, trained in pediatrics at Seattle Children's Hospital and completed subspecialty training in developmental behavioral pediatrics at Boston Medical Center. Her research interests include use of mobile technology by parents and young children and how this relates to child self-regulation and parent–child interaction. Clinically, her work focuses on developmental and behavioral problems in low-income and underserved populations. She was lead author of the 2016 American Academy of Pediatrics (AAP) policy statement on digital media use in early childhood.

Ellen Wartella researches the effects of media and technology on children and adolescents, and the impact of food marketing in the childhood obesity crisis. She is the Sheik Hamad bin Kalifa Al-Thani Professor of Communication Studies at Northwestern University. She holds courtesy appointments in the Department of Psychology, the Department of Human Development and Social Policy and the Department of Medical Social Sciences. The author or editor of 12 books and approximately 200 book chapters, research articles, technical reports and research papers, Wartella is currently Co-principal Investigator on a 5-year multisite research project entitled: "Collaborative Research: Using Educational DVDs to Enhance Young Children's STEM Education" (2014–2019) from the National Science Foundation. She is editor of *Social Policy Reports*, a journal of the Society for Research in Child Development. She is a fellow of the American Academy of Arts and Sciences, the American Psychological Society (APA) and the International Communication Association (ICA). She is also a past President of the International Communication Association. She received the Steven H. Chaffee Career Productivity Award from the ICA, the Distinguished Scholar Award from the National Communication Association and the Krieghbaum Under-40 Award from the Association for Education in Journalism and Mass Communication.

Foreword

Milton Chen

Senior Fellow, George Lucas Educational Foundation
Trustee, W.K. Kellogg Foundation

Long ago, in a presidency far, far away, Thomas Jefferson invited guests to dine at the White House and his Monticello home in a tradition now known as the Jeffersonian dinner. Guests shared a meal around a table and discussed a topic of importance in the arts, sciences, or humanities. Opinions were debated, minds were expanded and proposals were made to improve our fledgling democracy.

Today, democratic ideals are under siege, schools are struggling to dismantle factory models of learning and adults face uncertain employment in the face of automation. The internet and digital media have transformed every aspect of living, learning and earning in this century, offering untold possibilities for education, but also sowing seeds of racism and distrust.

Perhaps it's time to acknowledge that the digital environment is now as immersive, tangible and vital to life as the physical environment. Creating a sustainable future is becoming as urgent for our children's digital lives as the crises threatening our ecosystems, where extreme weather, air and water pollution and climate change are on the rise. As internet hacking, fake news and divisive social media have shown, the climate is changing for our digital world as well.

How might children and families not merely survive, but thrive in these shifting digital times? The natural environment is shaped by many policymakers, government agencies, corporations, universities, funders and nonprofits, but also by the daily actions of adults and children in their homes, schools and communities. Similarly, a broad range of stakeholders must now align around a common mission to use powerful digital technologies for healthy development and learning.

Exploring Key Issues in Early Childhood and Technology: Evolving Perspectives and Innovative Approaches, should inform that movement. In book form, it is reminiscent of a Jeffersonian dinner, with its editor, Dr. Chip Donohue, playing the role of host, inviting 16 key experts from the US, UK, and Australia, and stimulating their best thinking. He sets the table by reminding us that the challenges of creating a healthier media landscape are not new, but we can follow in the paths of brave trailblazers who came before us. In his essay, Dr. Donohue shows how, 50 years after the first broadcast of *Mister Rogers' Neighborhood*, the wisdom of Fred Rogers is as relevant today as it was then.

In keeping with the ground rules for a Jeffersonian dinner, these 16 offer no long-winded speeches or academic treatises, but clarify key issues and research findings in concise, highly digestible essays. They are professors, media makers, teachers, non-profit leaders, journalists and a physician. They are also realists, documenting the disappointing phenomenon of parents too distracted by their own devices to engage with their children, with or without digital media. They advise that, rather than issuing blame, we should strive to better understand today's parents and how texting with friends or listening to a favorite playlist might soothe their stresses – the smartphone as adult pacifier.

Several authors warn that a "double digital disadvantage" may exist when lower-income families with fewer devices and slower internet access relegate their children to consuming mindless entertainment instead of using media tools to produce their own content. Others credit their mentors – those teachers who guided them on their journeys of understanding – and propose that a new role of "media mentor" will be needed for this generation of parents and caregivers.

These experts are also storytellers, providing accounts of parents and children navigating this landscape in creative ways to propel their learning and relationships. There are many tasty bites here, such as how technology might be used to slow down, rather than speed up, the pace of life and learning. And how valuable learning expeditions can start with something as simple as children's questions about the world around them.

These stories reveal how young children, given exposure to coding, animation and 3-D printing, demonstrate skills far beyond traditional notions of what children of their age can do. And how the new generation of devices, interacting through speech rather than typing, enables preschoolers to talk to Siri and Alexa, their internet librarians. These authors confirm the prophecy of MIT's Seymour Papert, who served as a "media mentor" for many of them, when he said that technology could provide "wheels for the mind."

Dear Reader, you are hereby invited to attend this Jeffersonian dinner. (In fact, this tradition is being renewed at dinner tables for community engagement around the country.) Imagine yourself sitting at this distinguished table and how you might contribute to the conversation, as a researcher, teacher, media professional, activist, student, parent, or caregiver. You might simulate the culinary experience by reading this book alongside your favorite meal.

You might even consider hosting your own Jeffersonian dinner as a book club, inviting your friends and colleagues to break bread and share reactions. Interesting projects might emerge for how families and communities can create the better digital environment we deserve. What could be more important to our democracy than the environment of ideas our children are raised in?

In the interests of historical accuracy, I note that Thomas Jefferson was a slaveholder of more than 175 slaves, who prepared and served those dinners and enabled him to enjoy the comforts of his estate. I reference the Jeffersonian dinner as a forum for intellectual exchange rather than unduly honoring the man.

Spotlight on Innovation, Impact and Influence

Center for Digital Media Innovation and Diversity located in the Learning Technologies division of George Mason University's College of Education and Human Development, the Center for Digital Media Innovation and Diversity seeks to leverage the expertise of scholars and industry professionals to conduct research, design digital media products, and provide access to quality educational media for diverse audiences. For example, the Center has explored the Digital Lives of African American families, applied Game Design principles and practices to broaden the participation of diverse students in STEM disciplines and careers, and featured quality educational digital media products targeting and/or created by diverse populations. In addition to his scholarly activities, Dr. Kevin A. Clark applies his extensive expertise and wealth of experience to serve as a consultant to many children's media organizations. Learn more at https://cdmid.gmu.edu.

Center on Media and Human Development (CMHD) in the School of Communication at Northwestern University is directed by Dr. Ellen Wartella. The CMHD employs psychological, educational and communication theories to investigate traditional media, such as television and advertising, as well as new media, such as social media and apps. The Center conducts research exploring a variety of topics like educational learning, social interactions, advertising and health, within the intersection of children and media. Learn more at https://cmhd.northwestern.edu.

Children and Technology Research Group in the Centre for Research in Digital Education at Moray House School of Education, University of Edinburgh, conducts research, teaching and consultancy that explores the role of technology in the everyday lives of young children. The Research Group thinks it's important to know more about living and learning with technology, whether it's at home with their families and other caregivers, in settings such as preschools, schools and museums, or in and around their neighbourhood. Central to their work is exploring the role that adults – parent, carer, teacher, researcher, designer, or policymaker – can have in positively guiding children's interactions with technology and the role of design in supporting positive play and learning. Research themes include: Children and digital media in the home; digital play; embodied learning; digital media and STEM education; computational thinking; children and data; and emerging technologies. The outcomes of their research contribute to discussions about the place of technology in young children's lives, create richer learning experiences for children and others by informing the design process, provide insights that are valuable for parents and educators, and engage decisionmakers in understanding more about the ways in which technology can support learning. Learn more at www.de.ed.ac.uk/children-technology.

Children's Technology Review began first as a graduate school assignment in 1983, morphing into a commercial printed newsletter in 1993, with the objective of helping parents, teachers and librarians find software. Today it is an online database with over 17,000 reviews, plus a weekly email newsletter. It is available by subscription. Learn more at www.childrenstech.com.

Designing for Children's Rights Association is a global non-profit association aiming to set new standards when designing for children and adolescents. The association wants to build a better world by empowering designers to make ethical products and services that respect and secure children's rights, partnering with UNICEF as their main strategic companion. The first iteration of the Designing for Children Guide was created by 70-plus designers, psychologists, neuroscientists, health-care specialists, educators and children's rights experts – during a Talkoot, a 48-hour collaborative event in Helsinki, Finland from January 19th to the 21st, 2018. Since then the association has grown and continues its global efforts and collaborations, with colleagues worldwide. They work to create awareness about the importance of keeping children's rights in mind when building products and services, by giving practical tools for designers, as well as getting children, parents and the community involved. Learn more at http://designingforchildrensrights.org/.

Developmental Technologies Research Group (DevTech), directed by Professor Marina Umaschi Bers at the Eliot-Pearson Department of Child Study and Human Development, Tufts University, aims to understand how new technologies that engage in coding, robotics and making, can play a positive role in children's development and learning. Their research involves three dimensions: Theoretical contributions, design of new technologies and empirical work to test and evaluate the theory and the technologies. They create programming languages such as KIBO and ScratchJr as well as teaching materials and pedagogical strategies for the professional development of early childhood educators and community engagement. Their longtime commitment is to inspire sustainable and scalable evidence-based programs for young children that promote the learning of programming and computational thinking with a playful, developmentally appropriate approach. Learn more at http://sites.tufts.edu/devtech/.

DigiLitEY (digital literacy and multimodal practices of young children). Young children are growing up in highly technologized societies across Europe and DigiLitEY will develop an interdisciplinary network that enables researchers to synthesize existing research and identify gaps in knowledge in this area. This will help to avoid duplication, foster innovative avenues for future research and effectively advance knowledge in this area. The focus is on children aged from 0–8, an age group for which there has been comparatively little research in this area. This research involves participants from a wide range of disciplines including: Applied Linguistics; Childhood Studies; Children's Literature; Computer Science; Cultural Studies; Early Childhood Education; Information Studies; Language and Literature; Media Studies; Psychology; Sociological Studies. This interdisciplinary approach is essential to the construction of knowledge in this area. The network will also identify new methodologies for working with young children and provide a theoretical framework that captures the digital literacy experiences of the whole child (at home, school, library, kindergarten and so on) in a holistic and ethical manner. Learn more at http://digilitey.eu/about/.

Dubit Limited founded in 1999, is a global agency specializing in children, encompassing both a research consultancy and a digital studio. Dubit has been at the forefront of delivering insights into the lives of children from its onset and is proud to have worked on truly innovative projects that have brought high-quality play, learning, engagement, and entertainment to young people. Dubit has been commissioned and retained by some of the biggest global brands (e.g., Viacom, Lego, PBS, Mattel, Turner, National Geographic and Discovery Communications), as well as by emerging companies and platforms. Learn more at www.dubitlimited.com/.

Dust or Magic Institute is a refresher course in developmental theory in the context of the current market, held in an inn on the Delaware River every fall for nearly 20 years, for leading reviewers, digital designers and researchers. The demonstration-rich agenda makes it easy to share ideas and to receive honest feedback. Learn more at www.dustormagic.com.

EU Kids Online is a multinational research network. It seeks to enhance knowledge of European children's online opportunities, risks and safety. It uses multiple methods to map children's and parents' experience of the internet, in dialogue with national and European policy stakeholders. It has been funded by the *European Commission*'s *Better Internet for Kids* programme. Learn more at www.lse.ac.uk/media-and-communications/research/research-projects/eu-kids-online.

Fred Rogers Center for Early Learning and Children's Media at Saint Vincent College enriches the development of current and emerging leaders in the fields of early learning and children's media by supporting the professional advancement and mentoring of the next generations of Fred Rogers through the Early Career Fellows program; educational opportunities for undergraduate Fred Rogers Scholars; research and special collaborations by Rogers Center Senior Fellows; and resources and information on the developmentally appropriate use of media. Established in 2003 to carry forward Fred Rogers' important legacy, the Center is the official home of the Fred Rogers Archive as well as a straightforward, understanding and compassionate voice for the healthy social and emotional development of children from birth to age 8. An advocate for the positive potential of technology to support children, families, educators and caregivers, the Rogers Center enjoys many collaborative relationships with educational institutions, research centers and community organizations. Fred Rogers knew the inherent value of childhood, and the importance of strengthening all adults caring for children. The Center's work carries forward three themes that were central to Fred's life and career. They aspire to help children *grow on the inside, learn through relationships and give meaning to technology*. Learn more at www.fredrogerscenter.org.

George Lucas Educational Foundation, edutopia.org, Lucas Education Research based in the San Francisco Bay Area, is dedicated to transforming K-12 education so that all students can acquire and apply the knowledge, attitudes and skills necessary to thrive in their studies, careers and adult lives. Founded by the filmmaker and technology innovator George Lucas in 1991, GLEF take a strategic approach to improving K-12 education through two distinct areas of focus: edutopia.org and Lucas Education Research. edutopia.org is a trusted source shining a spotlight on what works in education. Through its short films, articles and web features, it helps educators adopt and adapt best practices in schools and out-of-school programs. edutopia.org advocates for six transformational strategies: Project-based learning (PBL); social and emotional learning; comprehensive assessment; teacher development; integrated studies; and technology integration. The site and its associated social media are used by several million educators around the globe each month. Lucas Education

Research (LER) works with university partners and research firms to conduct rigorous research on innovative classroom practices, such as PBL. Through well-designed PBL, students and teachers explore real-world problems and challenges as core curricula. Students learn collaboration skills and how to communicate, create and think critically, with the end result of deep and meaningful learning. LER has begun to report the results of its field research and publishes related white papers. Learn more at www.edutopia.org/about.

Global Family Research Project is an independent, entrepreneurial non-profit organization that supports all families and communities in helping children find success in and out of school. They create a worldwide exchange of ideas to further the understanding and implementation of anywhere, anytime learning for all. Since 1983, the team has provided leadership to promote strategies that build equitable pathways for children's whole development across all learning environments. Learn more at https://globalfrp.org/.

Global Kids Online is an international research project that aims to generate and sustain a rigorous cross-national evidence base in support of policy and practical solutions for children's well-being and rights in the digital age, especially in the Global South. It was developed as a collaboration among the London School of Economics and Political Science (LSE), the UNICEF Office of Research-Innocenti and the EU Kids Online network, with partners around the world. The project has three practical outcomes: A research framework and multimethod tool kit to enable researchers to conduct reliable and comparable national research with children and their parents on the opportunities, risks and protective factors of children's internet use; a growing, multicontinent network of researchers, research users and expert partners, extending national research capacity in countries where the internet is relatively new; an evidence base needed by policymakers and practitioners as they seek to strengthen children's rights in the digital age by maximizing opportunities for children to benefit while minimizing the risk of harm from using the internet and mobile technologies. Anyone may use the Global Kids Online resources under the Attributive Non-Commercial Creative Commons License (CC BY-NC). Learn more at www.globalkidsonline.net/.

Institute for Learning Sciences and Teacher Education (ILSTE) at Australian Catholic University (ACU) focuses on 21st century teaching and learning, diversity, innovation and engagement with improving learning outcomes. The mission is to engage in vigorous, socially relevant and ethically committed research to improve outcomes for children, teachers and the wider community. ILSTE is a national research institute hosting a team of eminent researchers and international scholars undertaking funded research studies with a range of government and industry partners. ILSTE connects research with policy and practice by providing a forum for researchers, scholars, policymakers and practitioners to collaborate and share evidence-based knowledge to enhance quality teaching and learning. Research is premised on the idea that education, health and wellbeing predicate life opportunities. Researchers undertake investigations that generate new knowledge in education and learning including cognitive and noncognitive aspects. ILSTE spans various disciplines but the common goal is to remove barriers to learning and thereby enhance social and economic participation of all. Learn more at https://lsia.acu.edu.au/about/.

MakEY (Makerspaces in the Early Years: Enhancing Digital Literacy and Creativity) explores the place of the rising "maker" culture in the development of children's digital literacy and creative design skills. Research projects have been undertaken in seven European countries (Denmark, Germany, Finland, Iceland, Norway, Romania and the UK) and the USA in which staff working in makerspaces (including Fab Labs) have collaborated with academics to identify the benefits and challenges of running makerspace workshops in both formal (nurseries and schools) and informal (museums and libraries) educational settings. The research team has worked in partnership with academics in Australia, Canada, Colombia and the USA, creating a global network of scholars who are working together to further understanding of the role of makerspaces in developing young children's digital literacy and creativity. Throughout this work, the emphasis is on listening to the voices of children and engaging them meaningfully as participants in the research process. Learn more at http://makeyproject.eu/.

Mediatech Foundation is a non-profit, library-based, free-public access technology center that has been serving families in Flemington, NJ since 2003. It is especially busy after school for homework help, 3-D printing, console games, VR experiences, tablets, reliable internet access and the support of friendly media mentors. Learn more at www.mediatech.org.

New America is a think tank and civic enterprise dedicated to renewing America by continuing the quest to realize the nation's highest ideals, honestly confronting the challenges caused by rapid technological and social change and seizing the opportunities those changes create. The Learning Technologies Project, which is housed in the Education Policy Program at New America, focuses on how to ensure that digital media and interactive tools are used to advance equity for young children, students and families, as opposed to exacerbating existing divides. Learn more at www.newamerica.org.

Personalised Stories Project investigated the benefits and limitations of personalisation in children's digital products, with a specific focus on personalised books. The project was funded by the Economic and Social Research Council between 2016 and 2018 and hosted by the UCL Institute of Education, UK. Learn more at www.ucl.ac.uk/ioe/departments-and-centres/departments/learning-and-leadership/personalised-stories.

Preparing for a Digital Future and Parenting for a Digital Future is a three-year research project on *Preparing for a Digital Future*, conducted by researchers in the Department of Media and Communications at the London School of Economics and Political Science (LSE) and supported by a grant from the MacArthur Foundation from 2014 to 2017. The research team, led by Professor Sonia Livingstone, working with Dr. Julian Sefton-Green and Dr. Alicia Blum-Ross, is undertaking a series of qualitative case studies to investigate how children and young people, along with their parents, carers, mentors and educators imagine and prepare for their personal and work futures in a digital age. The pace of recent advances in digital media – not to mention talk about smart homes, geolocation apps, driverless cars and the Internet of Things – leaves many parents and carers increasingly anxious about what these changes will mean for their children, now and in the future. Parents are left unsupported by the polarized public debate about the detrimental effects of "screen time" on the one hand, and the visions of digital media as offering radically new pathways to academic achievement, or self-expression, on the other. To aid parents and policymakers in assessing the available evidence, the team has written a policy brief and a series of blog posts about *Parenting for a Digital Future*, that focus on the current state of research on "screen time" including case studies from their own research. Learn more at http://blogs.lse.ac.uk/parenting4digitalfuture/.

Radesky Lab at the University of Michigan leverages cross-disciplinary collaborations to discover novel ways of measuring family media use. Using developmental psychology methods of laboratory-based experiments and video coding, they are creating novel coding schemes to capture the nuances of parent–child–tech interaction. With oversight from human–computer interaction researchers and computer engineers, they are pilot testing apps that provide objective, real-time data about how parents and children use mobile devices throughout the day. Finally, Dr. Radesky's research assistants try to capture the child's digital play experience by installing and playing every game or app used in their cohort studies, coding it for educational quality, gamification and commercial content. Using these approaches, they hope to understand more about the ways families use media in everyday life. Learn more at https://sites.google.com/umich.edu/radeskylab/home.

Sesame Workshop is a global non-profit whose mission is to help all young children grow smarter, stronger and kinder. Co-founded by educational media and philanthropic pioneers, Joan Ganz Cooney and Lloyd Morrisett in 1968, the Workshop's evidence-based programs now reach some 150 million children in over 150 countries across the globe. *Sesame Street* and other educational programs produced by the Workshop are developed with a unique research and design process which emphasizes innovation and continuous improvement, as well as an urgent focus on reaching the world's most vulnerable children. Recent efforts have focused on early literacy, gender equity, diversity and inclusion, and health promotion initiatives that have both local relevance and global power. Sesame Workshop and the International Rescue Committee recently received a $100 million grant from the MacArthur Foundation to launch the largest humanitarian aid and education effort for young children in history. Learn more at: www.youtube.com/watch?v=eM8tv3Tfz5w and www.youtube.com/watch?v=oFBbOYaUYpo.

Technology in Early Childhood (TEC) Center at Erikson Institute empowers early childhood educators and parents to make informed decisions about the appropriate use of technology with children to support learning and positive development. The TEC Center's mission is built on three pillars: Research, Practice and Communication. The TEC Center is conducting cutting-edge, applied research to scientifically understand the ways in which teachers are incorporating technology into early childhood classrooms, how technology can support children's STEM interest and learning, and how technology can be used as a tool to connect the home and school environment. The TEC Center is dedicated to connecting research to practice by providing professional development opportunities for teachers and administrators that support the positive use of technology in early childhood settings. Through professional development programs, the TEC Center strengthens educators' digital literacy skills and their ability to intentionally select, use, integrate and evaluate technology in the classroom and other early childhood settings based on research and carefully selected real-world examples. Finally, the TEC Center is a leader in communicating research results and best practices to practitioners, educators, researchers, industry leaders and policymakers. Through convenings, academic books, journal articles, blog posts and social media activity, the TEC Center is a leader in engaging and connecting those in the fields of technology, education and child development. Learn more at http://tec center.erikson.edu.

W.K. Kellogg Foundation (WKKF), founded in 1930 as an independent private foundation by breakfast cereal pioneer Will Keith Kellogg, is among the largest philanthropic foundations in the USA. Guided by the belief that all children should have an equal opportunity to thrive, WKKF works with communities to create conditions for vulnerable children so that they can realize their full potential in school, work and life. Learn more at www.wkkf.org.

Acknowledgments

Pulling together an edited volume like this one is a challenging task for the editor and the contributing authors. In this case, the contributors are all thought leaders and innovators in their respective fields. That means they were already overcommitted and too busy to say yes to my request, but they did any way. After editing three books, I've come to realize that it is the busiest and most in-demand authors who find the time to do the writing and editing, respond to email requests quickly and contribute at the highest level of quality – worthy of the title, "thought leader."

The results of their individual and collective efforts are the book of essays you hold in your hands now. I hope you enjoy reading their writings as much as I have. In their words you'll find affirmation, inspiration, provocation and more than a few gentle nudges to move your thinking and practice forward.

I have talked and written about the idea of media mentors for a number of years. I want to sincerely thank each of the contributing authors for being my media mentors. You have inspired and challenged me, and it has been a personal joy and professional highlight to assemble this collection with you. A very special thanks to: Lewis Bernstein; Marina Umaschi Bers; Warren Buckleitner; Milton Chen; Kevin A. Clark; Susan Edwards; Shuli Gilutz; Lisa Guernsey; David Kleeman; Natalia Kucirkova; Michael H. Levine; M. Elena Lopez; Sonia Livingstone; Jackie Marsh; Lydia Plowman; Jenny Radesky and Ellen Wartella. You have each put the "thought" in thought leader.

My work with young children and technology began back in the Apple IIe days, but since 2012 my publications, presentations and advocacy have been shaped by my work with the team at the Technology in Early Childhood (TEC) Center at Erikson Institute. It was an amazing journey between March of 2012 and December 2018. I'm so proud of the work we did together and the impact and influence the TEC Center achieved through our collective efforts. Thanks, and congratulations, to Alexis Lauricella, Director; Tamara Kaldor, Associate Director; and Jenna Herdzina, Program Manager. There is a lot of each of you in these pages. And thanks to Amanda Armstrong who helped get the TEC Center off the ground, to Katie Paciga who joined us as an Early Career Fellow for two years and to Kate Highfield who left a lasting impression on all of us in the short time she was at Erikson Institute as a visiting scholar. Thanks also to Jie-Qi Chen and the members of the Erikson Institute leadership team, faculty and DLCE team who supported my work and valued the contributions of the TEC Center.

I also need to acknowledge the contributions of the Fred Rogers Center staff, especially my friend and co-conspirator Rick Fernandes, former Executive Director, and Roberta Schomburg, Interim Executive Director, who I have partnered with since I became a Senior Fellow. I have been a Senior Fellow since 1999 and my work with the Center and in support of the legacy of Fred Rogers has been personally and professionally transformational. Much of the work on this book was completed during 2018, the "year of Fred Rogers," when the movie, biography, *Neighborhood* anniversary and media attention put the focus on Fred Rogers and *Mister Rogers*, as I describe in my essay, *Fred Rogers: The Media Mentor We Need to Navigate the Digital Age*. A special thanks to archivist Emily Uhrin for tracking down the citations and references for the quotes I used in my essay, and for playing such an influential role as the source of information and insights during the year of Fred.

Finally, I want to thank my family for understanding why I needed to take on another book and why working with this group of contributors has been such a great honor and awesome responsibility. Thanks to Maria Hill, Sarah-Maria Hill Donohue, Laura Kaitlin Hill Donohue and Andy Ortman for helping me see this through during a challenging year of personal and professional transitions. As I write these words, I'm looking out the window at the Utah mountains and the snow is falling. It's a beautiful scene and a perfect place to edit this book. What a luxury to put the finishing touches on this collective effort in such an amazing setting.

Chip Donohue
Park City, Utah

Abbreviations and Acronyms

AAP	American Academy of Pediatrics
ACU	Australian Catholic University
ALSC	Association of Library Services to Children
APA	American Psychological Association
CAI	Computer-Aided Instruction
CAL	Coding as Another Language
CES	Consumer Electronics Show
CMA	Children's Media Association
CMCH	Center on Media and Child Health
CMHD	Center on Media and Human Development
COST	European Cooperation in Science and Technology
CSM	Common Sense Media
CTREX	Children's Technology Review Exchange
DAP	Developmentally Appropriate Practice
DevTech	Developmental Technologies Research Group
DigiLitEY	Digital literacy and multimodal practices of young children
DML	Digital media literacy
DOE	Department of Education
ECA	Early Childhood Australia
EDC	Education Development Center
ESA	Entertainment Software Association Foundation
FCC	Federal Communications Commission
Fred Rogers Center	Fred Rogers Center for Early Learning and Children's Media at Saint Vincent College
GLEF	George Lucas Educational Foundation
GLRP	Global Family Research Project
HHS	Health and Human Services
ICA	International Communication Association
ICT	Information and Communications Technology

ILSTE	Institute for Learning Sciences and Teacher Education
ISTE	International Society for Technology in Education
LER	Lucas Education Research
LSE	London School of Economics
MakEY	Makerspaces in the Early Years: Enhancing Digital Literacy and Creativity
MIT	Massachusetts Institute of Technology
MOOC	Massive Open Online Courses
NAEYC	National Association for the Education of Young Children
NAMLE	National Association for Media Literacy Education
NETP	National Education Technology Plan
NSF	National Science Foundation
OBE	Order of the British Empire
OHCHR	Office of the High Commissioner for Human Rights
PBL	Project-based learning
PBS	Public Broadcasting Service
RCPCH	Royal College of Paediatrics and Child Health
STEM	Science, Technology, Engineering, Math
TEC Center	Technology in Early Childhood Center at Erikson Institute
UCD	User-Centered Design
UDL	Universal Design for Learning
UN OHCHR	United Nations Office of the High Commissioner for Human Rights
UNCRC	United Nations Convention on the Rights of the Child
UNICEF	United Nations International Children's Emergency Fund
UX	User experience
WKKF	W.K. Kellogg Foundation

Introduction

Powerful Ideas about Young Children and Technology: Thoughts from the Thought Leaders

Chip Donohue

Context Matters

For the past ten years I've had the privilege of working at Erikson Institute in Chicago, a graduate school in child development, as Dean of Distance Learning and Continuing Education and the Founding Director of the Technology in Early Childhood (TEC) Center. That means I approach my work as a child development specialist curious about technology, not a technologist interested in young children.

I've also been a Senior Fellow and Advisor of the Fred Rogers Center for Early Learning and Children's Media at Saint Vincent College, so Fred's approach to using the technology of his day, broadcast television and children's programming, as a tool to support relationships and social emotional development, is another critical lens through which I view technology and media in early childhood.

For three years, I was a co-author and member of the working group that wrote the NAEYC (National Association for the Education of Young Children) and Fred Rogers Center Joint Position Statement on *Technology and Interactive Media as Tools in Early Childhood Programs Serving Children from Birth through Age 8* (2012), and that process included a deep dive into the research and best practices at the dawn of the era of multitouch screens and mobile devices.

And along the way I've edited two books published by Routledge, *Technology and Digital Media in the Early Years: Tools for Teaching and Learning* (2015) and *Family Engagement in the Digital Age: Early Childhood Educators as Media Mentors* (2017), that have included contributions from 54 thought leaders in child development, early learning and children's media.

A number of authors who have written essays for this book have also contributed to one or both of the previous collections, including: Warren Buckleitner, Kevin A. Clark, Lisa Guernsey, David Kleeman, Michael H. Levine and M. Elena Lopez. Contributors to each of these books have been thought leaders who helped the field explore key issues in technology, encouraged the evolution of my own perspectives and deepened my appreciation for innovative approaches that contribute to what we know, and help us understand what we still need to know, about early childhood and technology. And the process continues now with the 16 thought leaders whose essays you are about to read.

So, my context matters. Add it all up and you'll understand why I still agree with the Joint Position Statement that, "Technology and interactive media are tools that can promote effective learning and development when they are used intentionally by early childhood educators, within the framework of developmentally appropriate practice to support learning goals established for individual children" (NAEYC & Fred Rogers Center, 2012).

The Crowd Has Spoken

Exploring Key Issues in Early Childhood and Technology: Evolving Perspectives and Innovative Approaches explores issues and opportunities at the intersection of young children, child development, early learning, technology and children's media. Sixteen thought leaders were invited to contribute essays that address key concepts and big ideas within the context of their work and their individual perspectives on how technology can and should impact childhoods.

I certainly could have come up with a list of authors to invite on my own – my media mentors – but I also turned to the people in my professional networks and social media groups for recommendations about who they wanted to hear from and what topics and issues were most important to them in their work. This "crowdsourcing" process helped me decide who to invite and what topics and issues to focus on in this book.

The individual authors invited to write essays for this book are experts in child development, early childhood education, teacher education, parent engagement, informal learning, research, media literacy, children's rights and designing children's media. Each is an influential thought leader in the international conversations around effective, appropriate and intentional use of technology in the early years. They bring years of experience and expertise to their writing and share a commitment to young children and child development first, technology second. The book reads like a master class. In these pages you have the opportunity to learn from the most influential and impactful educators and researchers who are moving the needle on what we know about emerging technologies and current issues for young children and their families in the digital age.

The group of contributing authors whose essays are included in this book truly are my media mentors and each has earned their reputation as a thought leader: Lewis Bernstein; Marina Umaschi Bers; Warren Buckleitner; Milton Chen; Kevin A. Clark; Susan Edwards; Shuli Gilutz; Lisa Guernsey; David Kleeman; Natalia Kucirkova; Michael H. Levine; M. Elena Lopez; Sonia Livingstone; Jackie Marsh; Lydia Plowman; Jenny Radesky and Ellen Wartella.

Each author was asked to write an essay about what we know and what we still need to learn about young children and technology through the lens of their own experience, work, research and their fears and hopes for the future. Each essay, then, is a personal reflection by the author on what they've learned, what they're working on now, where their work will go in the future and what they believe the intersection of young children and technology should look like and feel like.

Taken together the essays offer a remarkable look at young children and technology from these thought leaders, individually and collectively. As each of them reflects on their work, their contributions and what they are most interested in moving forward, you will be affirmed, encouraged, challenged, inspired, provoked and nudged in your own thinking, practices and relationships with young children and families.

Powerful Ideas: Thoughts from the Thought Leaders

A bit more context. My interest in technology and young children was sparked in the early 1980s by two events. The publication of *Mindstorms: Children, Computers and Powerful Ideas* by Seymour Papert in 1980 and, in 1984, when Apple IIe computers went into Woodland Montessori School in Madison, Wisconsin where I was the Director and the Preschool Lab at the University of Wisconsin-Madison where I was beginning my PhD program, and into my home for playing, learning and early days messing about.

Marina Umaschi Bers, who has contributed an essay on coding as another language, studied with, and was mentored by, Seymour Papert at the Massachusetts Institute of Technology (MIT) Media Lab. Papert's work with Jean Piaget led him from the constructivist approach to his own constructionist theory of development, and along the way his work influenced much of the work described in these essays. Papert wrote, "When one enters a new domain of knowledge, one initially encounters a crowd of new ideas. Good learners are able to pick out those which are powerful" (Papert, 1980, 137).

This book is a collection of powerful ideas and innovative approaches from the thought leaders who continue to lead the conversation about the appropriate and intentional use of technology and digital media in the early years. Some focus primarily on young children in their research and practice, while others are focused on teacher education and professional development. Some look at how new technologies can enhance communication and enhance family engagement efforts, while others are interested in children's rights, designing children's media or the impact of the connected world on the health and safety of young children. As you read the big ideas in their essays, I encourage you to "pick out those which are powerful."

A Roundtable on Children's Media

Imagine the powerful ideas that would flow from a group conversation with all of these contributing authors. If I had gathered them together for a roundtable conversation imagine what we would have heard and could have learned. As is often the case in a convening such as this, everyone would have something to add to the conversation.

Lewis Bernstein might ask the group to think about how to best provide "guidance to the producers, and pipeline and platform owners, about both their responsibilities and the opportunities they have to contribute to our nation's children and the future of this country?"

David Kleeman might offer a provocation that, "The concept of 'screen time' has become meaningless in a world where screens bring entertainment, learning, discovery, communication, play, creation and more." And Ellen Wartella might observe that, "We may find that the affordances of smartphones and tablets are especially helpful learning tools for young children." Warren Buckleitner could keep the conversation going by sharing his thoughts about the potential for technology to be a tool for communication and relationships, saying, "Mobile technology has made us the first generation of parents to be physically far from our grown children, but we have the capacity to be psychologically closer."

Sonia Livingston who focuses on children's rights in the digital age might add, "Children increasingly see digital technologies – along with the digital literacy, agency and privacy to use them – as their preferred (and sometimes only) way to access their fundamental human rights across the board." Kevin A. Clark, who studies issues of diversity in media, joins the conversation to offer his hope and a provocation, "Imagine what would happen if all children read books, saw television programs, watched movies, and played games that presented positive portrayals of people who look like them." And Michael H. Levine might add, "Kids' enthusiasm for digital activities presents a great 'hook' for teachers and busy parents to manage their responsibilities, but if educators and parents themselves do not become technically proficient, the full range of digital possibilities – and the access to new technological tools – will effectively be reserved for the more privileged." Lisa Guernsey, a frequent collaborator with Michael and a leader in the media mentor movement, might imagine that, "With ideas and guidance from media mentors, educators and parents can learn to take advantage of children's natural curiosity to build their critical thinking skills about all the message they see and hear."

M. Elena Lopez, an expert on family engagement and the intersection of new tools with proven strategies, might remind us that, "Family engagement is foremost a shared responsibility of parents and educators for children's learning. And pediatrician Jenny Radesky might add that, "Meeting parents *where they are* is essential for effective communication about difficult topics." Never one to miss a chance to talk about Fred Rogers, my nudge would likely be, "Fred was a mentor and role model to parents and caregivers about the importance of binging every part of who you are into your interactions and relationships with a child." And Elena could share her research that, "Families discover how to make the early literacy experience fun and developmentally appropriate; children learn together with their families among a community of caring people; and through digital media, families help librarians extend their influence beyond the library walls."

Not to be left out, a number of people are interested in talking about children's rights, media developers and design and the ways in which we conceptualize technology in the early years. Shuli Gilutz, could insist that "Designers must be keenly aware of the physical, cognitive, social and emotional development of the children they are designing for." Susan Edwards, whose focus is on understanding digital play, might remind us that educators need to be "Thinking about the digital as well as the play." Lydia Plowman, whose essay is about when technology disappears, might suggest that "Designing for young children in a world of ambient computing provides a wonderful opportunity to explore the ways in which technology can provide fun, pleasure and play." Jackie Marsh, who writes about makerspaces, might add that, "If we view digital literacy as a social practice in which children engage in meaning-making practices in order to express themselves and communicate with others, then it seems appropriate to extend the modes and media available for this to include new technologies, such as digital fabrication tools." Marina Umaschi Bers might share her conclusion that, "As more people learn to code and computer programming leaves the exclusive domain of computer science to become integral to other professions, it is more important than ever that we develop computer science pedagogies that promote deep and thorough engagement for everyone." Finally, Natalia Kucirkova, who writes about the need for balance between personalized education and technology, warns that, "If we used technology for motivational ends only, we might support children's learning interests but not necessarily their learning."

How wonderful it would be to hear from these thought leaders individually and collectively in real time. Instead, you have the opportunity to turn the page and begin reading the essays that include the quotes from the roundtable conversation. As you read their essays you'll learn about their work and perspectives, reflect on the applications and implications of their ideas on your own work and decide how you will respond to their provocations and nudges.

How This Book Is Organized

Essays from contributing authors, arranged as 17 chapters, make up this book. Each essay represents the ideas, accomplishments and aspirations of innovative thought leaders in child development, early childhood education, teacher education, research, children's media, public media, pediatrics and public policy. I encourage you to take the time to read their bios in the Contributors section, and the program and project descriptions in the Spotlight on Innovation, Impact, and Influence section, to appreciate their unique perspectives, hear their individual voices, understand the context of their work and to be inspired by the innovative approaches they are implementing.

As I was pulling this book together, I felt like a music producer choosing the order of tracks for a "greatest hits" compilation from the top artists of the day. The essays have been arranged like the songs on a CD, or a playlist on a streaming music service. Taken together, the topics of each essay tell individual stories and the book offers a wide range of issues and innovations that captures a moment in time in our understanding of what we know and what we still need to learn about young children and technology. You can read them from front to back or in any order based on your interest in specific topics or authors, much like listening to your playlist in order, listening to a favorite song first or selecting shuffle all. No matter how you decide to proceed, there is much to discover, reflect upon and learn from in each of the essays and from each of the contributing authors.

Opportunities to Dig Deeper and Learn More

A unique feature of this book is that at the end of many of the essays, the contributing authors were asked to share three lists with the readers:

1. "Essential" lessons learned and next steps for educators.
2. Selected readings and resources of their own work so you can learn more about what they've done, how they think and what matters most to them.
3. A list of recommended readings and resources by the thought leaders they most respect and turn to when they want to learn more and advance their own thinking, so you can begin to understand who and what has influenced their thinking and work.

At the end of the book you'll find a Learn More section with links to organizations, programs and projects mentioned by the authors in their bios and essays.

I can't invite you to our fictional roundtable, but on behalf of the contributing authors I encourage you to take the time to explore the topics, key concepts and big ideas presented in each essay, reflect on how the "essentials" can be implemented in your own practice, dig deeper into the body of work of each author and learn more about the other authors and programs they have recommended to deepen your knowledge and benefit most from what each contributor has offered.

References

National Association for the Education of Young Children & Fred Rogers Center for Early Learning and Children's Media at Saint Vincent College. (2012). *Technology and interactive media as tools in early childhood programs serving children from birth through age 8*. Washington, DC: NAEYC and Latrobe, PA: Fred Rogers Center for Early

Learning and Children's Media at Saint Vincent College. www.naeyc.org/content/technology-and-young-children.

Papert, S. (1980). *Mindstorms: Children, computers, and powerful ideas.* New York, NY: Basic Books.

Selected Resources

Donohue, C. (Ed.). (2015). *Technology and digital media in the early years: Tools for teaching and learning.* New York, NY: Routledge and Washington, DC: NAEYC.

Donohue, C. (Ed.). (2017). *Family engagement in the digital age: Early childhood educators as media mentors.* New York, NY: Routledge and Washington, DC: NAEYC.

Chapter 1

Media and Marriage
"From This Day Forward, for Better or for Worse"

Lewis Bernstein

From This Day Forward

An odious comparison – Media and Marriage. Or is it? One is supposed to be sacred. Wait: both can be; or unfortunately both can be profane.

When I first began working at *Sesame Street* as a young researcher I remember reviewing a draft of a particular script. I told one of the creative geniuses of *Sesame Street* that the script had no educational goal, no real joyful, redeeming entertaining value, no nothing. His response: "it's a goddam television show". I was in shock. After all, this was *Sesame Street* – so much more than just a television show. And then, after getting to know this talented artist better, I recognized he didn't really believe that, if he did he wouldn't be working there. He was just complaining about the process – the mandate that had young researchers and educators like me review and critique every (expletive, according to him) idea that he and the other writers were doing. Creatives and educators were indeed in a shotgun marriage for better or worse. We were in it together, despite complaints from both sides, of which there were many, as in every marriage.

Everyone who worked on *Sesame Street* knew it was much more than just a goddam television show. In fact, quite the opposite, most felt it was a sacred mission, a calling. It grew out of the culture of the late 1960s and the dreams that, as a country, we could engineer both rockets to the moon and a "head start" for all of our nation's preschool children. We believed we could raise the quality of education for all children through a medium that could reach into every home. A medium that had not been used in the main to educate. A medium that had been called a "vast wasteland" by Federal Communications Commission (FCC) Chairman, Newton N. Minow, in 1961.

And yet a medium that Joan Cooney, a creative documentary producer, and Lloyd Morrisett, a cognitive psychologist and foundation executive, decided to experiment with, because of its ubiquitous reach and its unexplored potential to deliver content of value to the nation's preschool children: especially those who were disadvantaged and unable to attend preschools, but who, in the main, had access to television in their homes. They believed presciently that television's powerful formats could provide opportunities to educate with action, song, drama and humor.

"We believed we could raise the quality of education for all children through a medium that could reach into every home. A medium that had not been used in the main to educate. A medium that had been called a vast wasteland."

In some ways, by taking on a heavily criticized medium, Joan and Lloyd were playing with fire. As Marshall McLuhan framed it: "the medium was the message" (1964), and the medium was considered a big negative. I remember when the Lubavitcher Rebbe was asked how he and his Ultra-Orthodox Chasidim could possibly dare to use the television medium to teach values – the very same tool that delivered violence and pornography to so many – he gave an answer still relevant today for producers and consumers of media, alike. The story has been told that he pointed to a knife on his desk saying:

> You see this knife – it can be used to cut challah on the Sabbath as an instrument of blessing, or God forbid it could be used as an instrument of violence. It is inherently neutral: it all depends on how it is used.

Responsibility begins with the creator/producer. This is something that most creators and producers are either oblivious to, want no part of, or deny. But there is no getting around that producers have a responsibility to own up to what they produce for future generations. We/they certainly take credit when awards are given out. We/they are not exempt from the negative impact of our productions and acts of creation.

Yet that responsibility is not the creators' alone; it is shared by others as well – parents, educators and even policymakers – who bear some responsibility about what content is allowed to enter our homes, schools, devices, and through them into the minds of our children. We all share responsibility to mediate our children's exposure to media. What content do we feel will support children's cognitive, emotional, social and moral development? What content is akin to food that is pernicious, and what is nutritious, and what is just acceptable as occasional junk food treats? How do we provide guidance and mediation for our children who are inundated with all too many options? How do we guide busy parents and teachers about children's screen time, and about the contents themselves? And how do we provide guidance to the producers, and pipeline and platform owners, about both their responsibilities and the opportunities they have to contribute to our nation's children and the future of this country?

These are some of the questions that I am concerned with in my post-*Sesame Street* years. My attention has shifted from television to the big platforms that reach so many of the world's children. These are the ubiquitous platforms of today, akin to the television medium when *Sesame Street* first began. Many of the executives I have met, at Facebook and elsewhere, are very aware of their responsibilities and are legitimately concerned about protecting children from the downside of media and the perils that can prey on them. But that is only half of the equation: the glass half-empty approach. My physician wife shared a basic premise of medicine with me when I first began working at *Sesame Street: primum non nocere* – first do no harm. But that's just a beginning – necessary but insufficient. Education and enlightenment is about more. Just as medicine is concerned with preventing as well as treating disease – it is also importantly concerned about wellness, nutrition, exercise and immunizations too. Big media and the big platforms, like Facebook, Google and Yahoo, Amazon, Netflix and others, need to be concerned about potential and opportunities, not only safety and protection, and damage control.

> **"... how do we provide guidance to the producers, and pipeline and platform owners, about both their responsibilities and the opportunities they have to contribute to our nation's children and the future of this country?"**

What do I advise big media based on what I have learned through my 40-plus years at Sesame? Below are four big ideas I learned working both sides of the creative/educator shotgun marriage that was *Sesame*. I recommend producers, parents, educators and policymakers alike think seriously and systematically about them all. Above all, I recommend they do their best to foster learning through joy, humor, play, adventure and safe, guided experimentation for all children; that they mine children's potential for agency, empowerment, creativity, expression and build children's ability and belief in themselves to change the world for the better. And I remind them that 40 years ago *Sesame Street* served as a window to the world for children, especially disadvantaged children who typically would not be exposed to those different from themselves, or places far away.

> **"I remind these mega media platforms that they have the unique opportunity today to introduce children to a diversity of people and cultures, ideas and perspectives from around the world and encourage learning about the 'other' while learning most importantly about themselves, our own nation's values, as well as timeless universal ones."**

Big media can do that too. *Sesame Street* provided virtual visits to museums to expose children to art created by the world's great artists, and music by the world's best musicians, and so I remind these mega media platforms that they have the unique opportunity today to introduce children to a diversity of people and cultures, ideas and perspectives from around the world and encourage learning about the "other" while learning most importantly about themselves, our own nation's values, as well as timeless universal ones.

Vision, Values and Zeitgeist

It all begins with a vision that takes into account the values that one feels are essential to convey to the next generation, especially during a particular zeitgeist – the social, cultural, educational and political climate of the times. Of course, one needs to convey the timeless universal values that transcend a particular zeitgeist. But being sensitive to the needs of a particular moment in time provides opportunity, and at times a readiness for acceptance that might not be available at another point in time.

In the late 1960s, when *Sesame Street* began, it was not only a time of the launching of rockets to the moon, but also a time of great cultural upheaval – protests against racism, protests against an unpopular war, the beginning of the Great Society programs: in short, a time of great experimentation. *Sesame Street*, too, was an experiment to see if the television medium could be used to educate. And, within the series, Sesame launched mini-experiments with new formats for television – short commercial-like segments purposefully intended to teach letters, words, numbers, mathematical concepts and more, instead of persuading consumers to purchase a particular product. The thinking: if Tony the Tiger could sell Frosted Flakes, short segments could be used to educate. The street scenes and live-action films were intentional too: to support a vision of pluralism, of harmony from diversity, modeling Blacks and Whites, a Jewish shopkeeper and an Hispanic fix-it shop owner, Muppets of all colors and temperaments, all living together on one street, listening to each other and resolving their clear differences with humor and, mostly, amicably.

What were those transcendent and timeless values that *Sesame Street* was conveying implicitly and explicitly?

- First and foremost, it was recognition of, respect for and an embrace of the richness of human diversity, with a social agenda for inclusiveness – whether that inclusiveness was of different races, economic strata, language groups, immigrants or native-born Americans, and/or level of ability or challenge.
- Second, was the message that everyone can learn, probably differently, with some formats and curriculum goals more appealing and easier for some, and others for others, leading us to try lots of different approaches.
- Third, learning can be and should be fun, so we integrated joy with learning, education with entertainment.
- Fourth since our whole *Sesame* endeavor was an experiment, the ultimate arbiters of our success or failure, of what would be included

and continued, was to be decided through research: what did our audience of children engage in and learn from best?

These issues are still relevant today, but given the current zeitgeist we need to go much further, by emphasizing civility, the need to listen to each other, especially to opinions that different from our own. We need not only to protect children from too much of anything that will pollute their brains – on whatever medium they may be using at the moment – but we need also, and maybe even more importantly, help children develop their own internal filters to distinguish between fact and fiction, truth from lies, something important from something trivial. We need to help children to also develop a sense of justice, fairness, compassion and a way to distinguish right from wrong. We cannot assume that children will develop these precious filters and even more precious values by osmosis: certainly, not from any political leadership. And we need to help children develop an understanding of how to manage and balance their time for maximum benefit on the continuity that for them consists of both online and off-line experiences.

"These issues are still relevant today but given the current zeitgeist, we need to go much further, by emphasizing civility, the need to listen to each other, especially to opinions that different from our own ... and help children to develop their own internal filters to distinguish between fact and fiction, a sense of justice, fairness, compassion and a way to distinguish right from wrong."

The Child, Family and Community

In his poem, "The Diameter of the Bomb", Yehuda Amichai (1996) describes the limited but lethal size of a bomb, and how its impact diffuses across the lives of those it wounds, and those relatives close by and far away perhaps on the other side of the world, and even God on his throne above. And what is the diameter of an education? It starts with an individual child with a unique character who – if we are good teachers – we help to learn first about who he or she is and who he or she can become, about developing his or her physical, cognitive, social and moral self. Then we help teach that child to relate to siblings, parents, family, friends and the other. What we teach has the potential to not only funnel inwards and enter a child's mind, heart and soul, but through media can also ripple outwards not only to the child's parents and siblings, but further into the world so much more widely. We media producers think about the masses who can be exposed to what we produce. But we need to begin by thinking about the unique characteristics of each individual child, his and her needs, abilities, tastes, as well as the collective universal values and contents that will help build that child's character to become a contributing member of a world he or she will lead into the future.

Tradition, Experimentation and Personal Responsibility

We know a lot about education and media. We need to transmit and build on what we know – both in terms of content and formats. But we also need to innovate and experiment with the formats of how we convey knowledge and allow our children to assimilate and share knowledge. At *Sesame Street* when we began, we knew a lot about modeling theory, associative learning and more. But how we put those theories into practice through the television medium demanded experimentation, which we did lots of, learning through empirical iterative research what worked and what didn't. We need a dose of that same kind of experimentation with the new tech tools of today that can allow for the different skills that we want our children to master. We would be wise to support both foundational learning of traditional skills in classic education as well as to experiment with new ways to transmit knowledge, legacy and values. We must not be afraid to embrace the unknown. Yet – as James Oberg a space engineer once said – "let's not be so open minded that our brains fall out" (Sagan, 1996, p. 187). We have a responsibility to be vigilant and mediate how and how much our children use these wonderful new tools. We need to remember and take greater advantage of the fact that education is not confined to the limited time our children spend in the classroom. I remember when our eldest daughter had her first playdate with a neighbor's child. The father asked me a question about what my child was learning, and I told him I wasn't sure, but I trusted her excellent teacher. He responded: are you going to leave the education of your child to her school alone? That comment struck a deep chord. You mean I now had to do something too? I was now on the line, responsible, no longer fully comfortable delegating the education of my child just to her school.

What does that mean today for all of us who are so busy with all the opportunities and risks of the world in front of our children though all the media they are exposed to: books, television, computers, iPads, cell phones and whatever is next? It means that we can't shirk our personal responsibility to provide guidelines to our children's virtual lives just as we have that responsibility for their "off-line" lives, whether they be in school, at home, at play or anywhere. We – producers, consumers, teachers, policymakers alike – all are on the line – we all share responsibility for the education of our next generation.

The Message, the Medium, the Magic and the Marriage

In Hollywood, Sam Goldwyn – or some say Moss Hart – said movies aren't about messages and content. "If you have a message, call Western Union", one or the other of them famously said. Movies were meant to be magic, fantasy, adventure, romance. Could *Sesame Street* integrate messages as well as magic through the television medium? If it were up to the educators and researchers on *Sesame Street* we would likely have just focused on the educational content. And if it were up to the creative writers and producers, they would have focused only on the entertainment. Perhaps that was one of the most important ideas that Joan Cooney and Lloyd Morrisett shared: insisting that every *Sesame Street* segment have an educational goal as the kernel within a shell of stellar artistic entertainment. To do that, they hired educators and researchers to work with comedy writers and entertainment producers, forcing us to work together. At first the shotgun marriage was rocky: what do you mean we had to use the word "cooperation" in this segment, they would ask? That's the goal we answered, and you need to provide the term, the conceptual peg upon which children could hang different examples of cooperative activity on. Give me a break, they would answer. And then, over time, the curriculum the educators produced served as the framework around which the writers weaved their creative mini-masterpieces. We all knew, that when education was well integrated within the entertainment, we had produced a successful segment. If we had blended joy with learning, education with entertainment, we knew we were on the road to impact. We demanded that the series provide children with both artistic and educational excellence, and combine the two. We sweated over every detail: could we teach children about body parts by introducing them to a Picasso painting and labeling the parts of the face? Could we introduce children to diversity and the concepts of ability and disability and tangentially introduce some to classical music perhaps for the first time with violinist Itzhak Perlman? Yes, we could. And when we got it right, it was indeed magical, making learning cool and joyful.

Part of that magic was what one of our producers called *Sesame Street*'s sensibility: always trying to provide excellence and quality, but more importantly, never talking down to children; always treating them with the respect they deserved and that we wanted them to show to others. It is something that the show's marriage partners struggled with, successfully in the main, for close to 50 years. And it is a legacy for producers, parents and teachers, to aspire to think about how they too can work to integrate joy with learning, humor with guidelines, whether that learning be at home, in the car on the road or in the classroom.

I conclude with the following hope: may we all be wise and good-humored as we educate, nurture and love our children, in each and every medium they come upon, and most especially, up close and personal.

Lewis' Essentials

1. **Vision, Values and Zeitgeist.**
2. **The Child, Family and Community.**
3. **Tradition, Experimentation and Personal Responsibility.**
4. **The Message, the Medium, the Magic and the Marriage.**

References

Amichai, Y. (1996). *The selected poetry of Yehuda Amichai (Revised, Expanded, Subsequent Edition). (C. Bloch & S. Mitchell Trans.).* Berkeley, CA: University of California Press.

McLuhan, M. (1964). *Understanding the media: The extensions of man.* New York: Mentor.

Sagan, C. (1996). *The demon-haunted world: Science as a candle in the dark.* New York: Ballantine Books. p. 187.

Chapter 2

Five Things That Haven't Changed (Much)

David Kleeman

I've been working in children's media since the early 1980s and studying it since the '70s. When I started, Amazon was a river and Apple was a snack. Phones were dumb and wired to the wall, and you took tablets for a headache. A virtual world was a couch fort, and the breadth of your social network depended on whether you were allowed to cross the street.

Clearly, much has changed since, mostly defined by the watershed advent of digital media. We've even coined terms for those who grew up before and after the arrival of interactive media – digital natives and digital immigrants.

Beneath the surface, though, how much has truly changed? Has ubiquitous computing altered children's development? People often talk about new technologies "changing the brain," but doesn't everything during early childhood? Neural connections are formed and pruned constantly in response to new experiences.

Instead, I would contend that technology alters the *context* under which children grow, learn and engage. In the documentary, *Won't You Be My Neighbor?* Fred Rogers is quoted as saying "the outside world of the child changes, but the inside of the child never changes" (Grierson, 2018). External shifts disguise much that remains constant, but here are five things that haven't changed (much) in the last 35 years.

1. **Classic play patterns endure, even on new platforms**
   Toy rotary telephones of yore have morphed into play smartphones, but their fundamental purpose remains to let toddlers model adults' behavior. Toca Boca often calls its apps "toys," because they are open-ended and imagination-fueled, with no right or wrong way of playing. In "creative" mode, Minecraft is akin to having a bottomless box of building bricks. Early AI-enabled dolls have failed, in part, because embedded electronics inhibit classic doll play, like bathing. At the New York Toy Fair, "Tech Toys" used to have a distinct section featuring a diverse mix of robots, do-it-yourself kits, kid tablets, mobile apps, responsive dolls and more. Now, most companies have integrated their

tech-enabled toys into areas grouped around a particular play pattern. They've realized that toystore owners don't ask for more chips and wires, but for games and toys that trigger timeless play instincts. Equally, when a parent goes shopping, they compare a digital art kit with paints and markers, not with robots. It does seem, though, that ubiquitous interactivity has led children to expect toys and games that offer them agency, dynamic and social experiences.

> **"... toystore owners don't ask for more chips and wires, but for games and toys that trigger timeless play instincts."**

2. **Kids still play with toys**
   Interestingly, they often do so in parallel with screen use. They bring action figures or "plush" to the television or tablet, and retell or extend stories, playacting favorite characters alongside what's happening on screen. Where digital and physical experiences combine, it seems there's been a recent shift. Initial generations of connected toys put the screen between the child and the toy (move the ball by touching the screen); now, more products invite the child to play with the toy, with the screen providing background or context (throw the ball, and the screen will tell you how fast it went).

3. **Kids still – always – crave stories**
   Every new medium brings new modes of storytelling, but they don't replace those that came before. Instead, today's children have the opportunity to be immersed in stories. Beyond movies, video and games, there's a revival of audio: books, podcasts and even stories from smart speakers. Some fear that these new vehicles are "outsourcing" parenting, but that's not new. My children grew up with a Fisher-Price cassette player ready to tell a favorite tale, when I wasn't available. Going forward, I'm particularly excited by the potential of augmented reality to "tag" the world with stories – including children's own narratives – rooted in place. Imagine walking down a street and having your phone buzz, to let you know that a story happened there, and being able to see it, projected in words and images.

4. **Television – linear video – is very much alive**
   Since the internet arrived, there's been handwringing about the death of television. Yet, three decades in, kids still spend the plurality of their media time with video – from million-dollar series, to toy unboxing, to live gamer "play-by-play." While viewing is increasingly on mobile devices, big screens are re-energized as well, now that "smart televisions" offer seamless access to Netflix, YouTube and more.

5. **Schedules survive; who controls them has changed**
   Today's children live in a "what I want, when I want it" world. If you

want to confuse a toddler, try explaining that her favorite show isn't on right now. Still, for many young people, the only way to make sense of too much choice is self-scheduling. We see consistent use patterns developing across both platforms and content. These appear to be based on the ebb and flow of children's days, taking into account time available, what they've been doing or will soon be doing, and emotional state. Suddenly, media companies are reconsidering the benefits of predictable services – YouTube advises its creators to post new videos on regular days and times.

> **"The concept of 'screen time' has become meaningless in a world where screens bring entertainment, learning, discovery, communication, play, creation and more."**

Innovator Alan Kay is purported to have said that "technology is anything that was invented after you were born." In the same way that my generation takes electric appliances for granted, today's children have never known a world that isn't customized, interactive, on-demand and mobile.

Ideally, children shouldn't have to think about technology. Done well, digital elements of play can become transparent. That's the challenge to content creators: to ensure that the inner workings recede into the background so that kids see only the magic, and know only that a story, game, app or toy taps their innate love for engagement, learning and fun.

David's Essentials

None of this is to say that digital technologies haven't brought about major changes, full of both opportunities and challenges:

1. **The concept of "screen time" has become meaningless in a world where screens bring entertainment, learning, discovery, communication, play, creation and more.** Teaching moderation and media literacy hasn't necessarily kept pace with the fire hose of content.
2. **Being "spoiled for choice" and the amount of free and easily accessed content can result in more sampling and fewer deep interactions.** Would we place more value on quality play experiences if they cost us more in time or money?
3. **Where once data collection meant a Nielsen diary, today every click and tap is harvested, analyzed and put to use.** Sometimes to provide personalized learning but sometimes to sell to children and invade their privacy.

4. **Digital media's global reach upends the concept of community.**
   Every child can find others who shares his or her passions, beyond the
   immediate neighborhood that used to limit their reach. On the other
   hand, they can't always know that their "friends" are who they purport
   to be; their reach may exceed their grasp.

References

Grierson, T. (2018). Mr. Rogers and why kind men freak us out. *MEL*. Available
online at https://melmagazine.com/en-us/story/mr-rogers-and-why-kind-men-
freak-us-out.

Learn More about David's Work

- Dissecting Technology Addiction, June 2018, DigiLitEY conference,
  Riga, Latvia. www.youtube.com/watch?v=ckCbkMBqFA0&t=763s.
- kidscreen profile. http://kidscreen.com/author/dkleeman/
- *One Mission, Many Screens: A PBS/Markle Foundation Study on Distinct-
  ive Roles for Children's Public Service Media in the Digital Age* (2002).
  www.markle.org/sites/default/files/omms.pdf
- "What Would Fred Rogers Say?" with Alice Wilder in *Technology and
  Digital Media in the Early Years: Tools for Teaching and Learning*, edited
  by Chip Donohue (2015).

David Recommends

- *Children and Television: Lessons from Sesame Street*, Gerald S. Lesser.
- *Tech and Play: Exploring Play and Creativity in Pre-Schoolers' Use of Apps*,
  Dubit and the University of Sheffield.
- *The Art of Screen Time: How Your Family Can Balance Digital Media and
  Real Life*, Anya Kamenetz.
- *Screen Time*, Lisa Guernsey.

Chapter 3

Fred Rogers

The Media Mentor We Need to Navigate the Digital Age

Chip Donohue

In 2009, before the *TEC Center at Erikson Institute* was launched, I became a Senior Fellow at the *Fred Rogers Center for Early Learning and Children's Media* in Latrobe, Pennsylvania. Since then I've had many opportunities to reflect on and share some of the timeless lessons Fred Rogers continues to teach parents, caregivers, educators and children's media developers as a broadcast television age media mentor for the digital age. In this essay I connect the dots between the lessons I've learned and the guidance I can offer for the grown-ups in young children's lives.

Mister Rogers' Neighborhood was produced in an analog age, but Fred's thoughtful, intentional and developmentally informed words and approach to children's media are still remarkably timely and contemporary. They offer essential guidance for families, educators and children's media developers who are helping young children safely navigate the digital age.

Fred Rogers was intentional about all he did so he consistently and authentically modeled the importance of studying and applying child development theories and emphasizing social emotional learning. He modeled interactions and relationships; consistent routines; moving at a child's pace; allowing pauses so the child has time to respond and grown-ups can listen; looking directly into the camera and speaking to one child at a time; and always keeping the children first. He held himself and those around him to high standards because, for Fred, nothing less than his best would do for the children who would watch and listen.

While his media and artistic outlet was broadcast television, today's media creators and the grown-ups in children's lives can follow Fred's lead and implement these simple and powerful ideas by embracing the technology and interactive media of our day to support healthy development and early learning and strengthen and engage families through intentional and appropriate use in the early years. "He used the cutting-edge technology of his day, television, to convey the most profound values – respect, understanding, tolerance, inclusion, consideration – to children".(King, 2018, p. 12).

Fast-forward to 2018 and what was undeniably the "year of Fred Rogers." Renewed interest in Fred Rogers and *Mister Rogers' Neighborhood* offered evidence that his groundbreaking work continues to inspire and inform us. In 2018:

- The 50th anniversary and 895 episodes of *Mister Rogers' Neighborhood* were honored and celebrated.
- Twitch.tv hosted a marathon of *Neighborhood* episodes to commemorate his 90th birthday on its streaming video platform.
- PBS aired a tribute, *Mister Rogers: It's You I Like.*
- Morgan Neville's documentary film, *Won't You Be My Neighbor?* struck a chord with audiences across the country.
- Maxwell King published an insightful biography, *The Good Neighbor: The Life and Work of Fred Rogers.*
- The US. Postal Service issued a commemorative *Mister Rogers* stamp.
- Contributing author Warren Buckleitner taught a course for media students, *The Methods of Fred Rogers*, at the College of New Jersey.
- The NAEYC Annual Conference opening session featured a panel discussion with Joanne Rogers, Bill Isler, Nicholas Ma and Junlei Li, "Reflecting on the legacy of Fred Rogers."

His comforting words, "Look for the helpers," and his Senate hearing testimony that "saved public television" reappeared frequently in social media as reminders of his lasting influence and impact in the *Neighborhood* and beyond.

Fred Rogers was a student of child development. He always focused on the whole child and everything that makes each child unique. He recognized that whole children need whole adults in their lives, and he demonstrated that belief every day. Fred was a mentor and role model to parents and caregivers about the importance of bringing every part of who you are into your interactions and relationship with a child. The whole and wholly authentic Fred Rogers was a musician, an ordained minister, a child development specialist, a parent and a beloved children's television innovator by being himself and being true to himself – Fred Rogers was Mister Rogers. Mister Rogers was Fred Rogers.

> **"Fred was a mentor and role model to parents and caregivers about the importance of bringing every part of who you are into your interactions and relationships with a child."**

His familiar song, "Won't you be my neighbor?" was, and still is, an invitation to children and adults to become a friend and neighbor. And in the neighborhood, he modeled experiences with technology that invited interactions, conversations and shared experiences intended to build and strengthen relationships between a young child and a caring adult. Media creators would do well to reflect on the many ways Fred invited children into his world, kept them safe, offered consistent routines, offered caring interactions, built relationships and based his content on what he knew about child development and early learning.

One of Fred's gifts to all of us was his unconditional acceptance and affirmation – he liked us just the way we are. He understood that parents, caregivers and early childhood educators are not unequipped to guide children through the digital age, but they often feel ill-equipped. In Fred's strengths-based approach, built on mutual respect and trust, he encouraged the grown-ups in a young child's life to understand and value what they do know and learn what they can do, instead of telling them what they don't know and what they can't or shouldn't do.

"He understood that parents, caregivers and early childhood educators are not unequipped to guide children through the digital age, but they often feel ill-equipped."

In my work with technology-mediated family engagement strategies, I have tried to follow Fred's example by providing simple and actionable messages to parents and caregivers that affirm, encourage, engage, empower and gently nudge them to be media mentors for young children. I can't help but think that he would have been troubled by how digital-age grown-ups are struggling to manage their smartphones and are always on screens, resulting in the rise of "present without presence" adult–child interactions.

Anyone who ever met Fred tells the same story about how he was fully present, focused only on the person he was talking to at the time and how genuinely interested he was in what you had to say. I know, I experienced this for myself in 1994 in a crowded and noisy exhibit hall at the NAEYC conference in Anaheim, California. In my brief encounter, Fred transformed me from someone in the crowd to the most important person at that moment. It wasn't just what he said, it was how attentively he listened to my story. How can we help digital-age adults to put down the phone, turn off the screen and be present with presence – so that the young child with them experiences what it means and how it feels to interact with an adult who is engaged, tuned in and attentive?

Fred also encouraged grown-ups to hold on to their "childlikeness" to better see the world through the eye of a child. For example, to remember what it felt like as a child to wake up and look out of the window at a freshly fallen blanket of snow, not just what it feels like as an adult to see the same beautiful snow but think only about shoveling the driveway, driving on slippery roads and how long it is going to take to get to work.

Fred Rogers said, "I love whimsy, don't you? If you're going to be working for children, you need to do your best not to lose your childlikeness. It's wonderful to be able to just be yourself" (Wedlan, 1997).

Fred never lost his love of whimsy and "childlikeness." He modeled many ways to keep the inner child alive, and one of my favorite quotes and gentle reminders from him is "The child is in me still ... and sometimes not so still." (Rogers, 2003, p. 26). What a "gift that keeps on giving" it is to a young child when an adult enters their world, shares their interests, sees the world through their eyes, joins in playfully and follows their lead.

Fred Rogers identified six "essentials" that he believed every child needs to experience for healthy growth, development and learning. This list also provides a recipe for grown-ups who are raising or educating young children and children's media developers who are designing technology and media for children.

Fred Rogers' 6 Necessities for Learning

1. A sense of self worth
2. A sense of trust
3. Curiosity
4. Capacity to look and listen carefully
5. Capacity to play
6. Times of solitude

(Rogers & Head, 1983)

Despite an award-winning career in children's television, Fred always knew it was not about the technology. What matters most is relationships. Technology can be a tool to bring people together and help them communicate with one another as long as today's interactive media includes interactions with others.

Fred Rogers said, "Love is at the root of everything – all learning, all parenting, all relationships. Love or the lack of it. And what we see and hear on the screen is part of who we become" (from the documentary, *Fred Rogers: America's Favorite Neighbor*, Family Communications, Inc. & WQED, 2003, as used in the film, *Won't You Be My Neighbor?* Capotosto, Ma & Neville, 2018).

Whatever role you play in the life of a young child, you matter. Be a positive role model, enthusiastic guide and mindful media mentor to help children safely navigate the digital age. Invite, encourage and empower other grown-ups to become role models and "helpers" in your neighborhood. Start with what you know, understand what matters most, consider what it means to be a good neighbor today and embrace your role as a media mentor.

What a difference you make, you who serve children and their families so directly! And they're so well served when they can come to believe that there isn't anything in their lives that can't be expressed in words or play or craft or whatever healthy way they happen to choose – Such a gift will last them all of their days. (Rogers, 1994a, p. 33)

In 2015, I wrote,

> Perhaps it is the blending and balancing of interactive technology and interactions with others that offers the most promise for effective and appropriate uses of technology in the early years – closely connecting Fred Rogers' approach with our emerging understanding of appropriate and intentional use of digital media to support early learning.

in the introduction of my book, *Technology and Digital Media in the Early Years: Tools for Teaching and Learning in the Early Years* (Donohue, 2015, p. 3).

Following the year of Fred Rogers, it is time to drop the "Perhaps" and all agree that interactive technology plus interactions with others – relationships – will always matter most.

Chip's Essentials: With Affirmation, Encouragement and a Gentle Nudge from Fred Rogers

1. Never forget that relationships matter most.

> Let's not get so fascinated by what the technology can do that we forget what it can't do ... It's through relationships that we grow best and learn best. (Sharapan, 2012, May)

2. Use media together to enhance learning and encourage interactions.

> Nothing will ever take the place of one person actually being with another person. There can be lots of fancy things like TV and radio and telephones and Internet, but nothing can take the place of people interacting face to face. (Davis, 2000, Interview with Fred Rogers)

3. Don't let technology displace or replace early childhood essentials like play and time outdoors.

> We have to help give children tools, building blocks for active play. And the computer is one of those building blocks. No computer will ever take the place of wooden toys or building blocks. But that doesn't mean they have to be mutually exclusive. (Kleeman, 2013)

4. Help children progress from just consuming media to also creating it.

> The very best kinds of playthings are open-ended. Children can make of them whatever they're working on at that moment, and their play is then determined by their own needs. (Rogers, 2002, p. 22)

5. **Use digital tools to empower grown-ups and enhance family engagement.**

Strengthen a parent ... and you strengthen a child. (Rogers, 1994b)

6. **Be a media mentor.**

I wanted (children) to know that I could use the computer, but that I could also turn it off. It takes a strong person to be able to turn off the computer. (Davis, 2000, p. 29)

References

Capotosto, C., Ma, N., & Neville, M. (Producers) & Neville, M. (Director). (2018). *Won't you be my neighbor?* [Motion picture]. Listed in Los Angeles, CA and New York: Focus Features.

Davis, J. (2000, October). Face time: Class acts. *Grok*, 26–36.

Donohue, C. Ed. (2015). *Technology and digital media in the early years: Tools for teaching and learning in the early years.* New York: Routledge and Washington, DC: NAEYC.

Family Communications, Inc. & WQED. (2003). *Fred Rogers: America's favorite neighbor.* Pittsburgh, PA: FCI and WQED.

King, M. (2018). *The good neighbor: The life and work of Fred Rogers.* New York: Abrams Press.

Kleeman, D. (2013, February 14). Beyond screen time [Fred Rogers Center Blog]. Retrieved from www.fredrogerscenter.org/2013/02/beyond-screen-time/.

Rogers, F. (2003). *The world according to Mister Rogers: Important things to remember.* Pittsburgh, PA: Family Communications, Inc.

Rogers, F. (2002). *The Mister Rogers parenting book.* Pittsburgh, PA: FCI and Philadelphia, PA: Running Book Publishers.

Rogers, F. (1994a). *You are special: Words of wisdom from America's most beloved neighbor.* New York: Penguin Books.

Rogers, F. (1994b). That which is essential is invisible to the eye. *Young Children 49* (51), p. 33.

Rogers, F. & Head, B. (1983). *Mister Rogers talks with parents.* Pittsburgh, PA: Family Communications, Inc.

Sharapan, H. (2012, May). *Professional development newsletter.* Pittsburgh, PA: Fred Rogers Company.

Wedlan, C. A. (1997, October 20). Can you say, "avid swimmer"? *Los Angeles Times.*

Learn More about Chip's Work

Donohue, C. (2017, November 13). PAST FORWARD: Reflections and visions on young children and technology [Fred Rogers Center Blog]. Retrieved from www.fredrogerscenter.org/2017/11/past-forward-reflections-visions-young-children-technology/

Donohue, C. Ed. (2017). *Family engagement in the digital age: Early childhood educators as media mentors.* New York: Routledge and Washington, DC: NAEYC.

Donohue, C. Ed. (2015). *Technology and digital media in the early years: Tools for teaching and learning in the early years.* New York: Routledge and Washington, DC: NAEYC.

Donohue, C. & Schomburg, R. (2017). Technology and interactive media in early childhood programs: What we've learned from five years of learning, research and practice. *Young Children* 72(4), pp. 72–74.

Paciga, K. & Donohue, C. (2017) *Technology and interactive media for young children: A whole child approach connecting the vision of Fred Rogers with research and practice.* Latrobe, PA: Fred Rogers Center for Early Learning and Children's Media at Saint Vincent College and Chicago, IL: Technology and Early Childhood Center at Erikson Institute.

Chip Recommends

Barr, R., McClure, E. & Pariakian, R. (2018). *Screen sense: What the research says about the impact of media on children aged 0-3 years old.* Washington, DC: Zero to Three.

Capotosto, C., Ma, N. & Neville, M. (Producers) & Neville, M. (Director). (2018). *Won't you be my neighbor?* [Motion picture]. USA: Focus Features.

Early Childhood Australia (ECA). (2018). *Statement on young children and digital technologies.* Canberra, ACT: ECA. http://dx.doi.org/10.23965/ECA.001

King, M. (2018). *The good neighbor: The life and work of Fred Rogers.* New York: Abrams Press.

NAEYC & the Fred Rogers Center for Early Learning and Children's Media at Saint Vincent College. 2012. *Technology and interactive media as tools in early childhood programs serving children from birth through age 8.* Joint position statement. Washington, DC: NAEYC and Latrobe, PA: Fred Rogers Center for Early Learning and Children's Media at Saint Vincent College.

Rogers, F. (1994). *You are special: Words of wisdom from America's most beloved neighbor.* New York: Penguin Books.

Chapter 4

Smartphones and Tablets and Kids – Oh My, Oh My

Ellen Wartella

Much has been written about the recurring public controversies about children and media going back to the 19th century and the rise of penny newspapers (Wartella & Reeves, 1985). Across the 20th century, public concerns about movies, radio, television and video games sparked similar arguments about the fact that children and adolescents were spending too much time on these media and that the content was inappropriate (i.e., too sexualized, too violent or too commercial) (Wartella & Robb, 2008). Over time, the academic literature examining the influence of these technologies found that their influence depended on the age of the child, the specific content the youth were attending to and the social context that might ameliorate the impact (such as having adults mediate via co-engagement with the child).

In recent years, while advisory groups such as the American Academy of Pediatrics (2016) recommend limiting young children's use of screen media (televisions, smartphones, tablets), it has been the case that children's use of screen media has increased (Rideout, 2017). Tablets and smartphones now dominate the technologies available to children and parents alike. While the majority of American homes acquired television sets by the 1960s, this newer form of digital technologies of smartphones and tablets, seems to me to be different from earlier generations of media technology. In this essay, I argue that smartphones and tablets may be game changers where young children are concerned.

First, the adoption of digital technologies has been rapid and ubiquitous. Rideout (2017) in a national survey for Common Sense Media reports that nearly all American children under eight today live in a home with a tablet or smartphone. This is a steep increase from a national population survey of parents of children aged eight and younger conducted in 2013 which found 69% of the families had smartphones and only 40% had tablets (Wartella et al., 2013).

Moreover, young children are having access to these technologies not just at home but in schools. There has been a steep increase in the use of tablets in schools with Apple reporting in 2013 that 4.5 million iPads were in American schools (Wartella et al., 2013). Beyond their ubiquity, both smartphones and tablets are quite different from earlier media in several important ways which have implications for child development.

First, touchscreen media are much easier for young children to manipulate than the more traditional televisions or even computers. Even a cursory look at YouTube videos shows very, very young children (under age one and often barely able to sit up) swiping across tablet screens. Very young children's use of both tablets and smartphones is often encouraged by parents and caregivers (Wartella et al., 2013) and now children have access to voice agents on smartphones (in addition to in-home devices such as Amazon Echo and Google Home) which makes it even easier for young children to use these technologies.

Further, in that 2013 survey of parents, for instance, we found that parents report giving their children these technologies to free themselves to do other things while the child is engaged (such as chores around the house or eating in restaurants) (Wartella et al., 2013). Moreover, parents report little frequency of co-engagement with the technology and their child. 29% of parents report playing with the smartphone with their child and 21% doing so on an iPad or tablet. This type of joint media engagement decreases especially for children over six years of age (for children aged six to eight in the survey, only 13% of parents reported that when their child was using a smartphone the parent was doing so along with the child "all or most of the time"; and 11% reported joint engagement with tablets). This is not that surprising when one considers the positive ways parents of young children view these digital technologies. Again, from the 2013 survey, parents of children aged eight and younger do not express much concern about their children's use of media technologies: 25% of parents of children under two are concerned compared with 36% of parents of six- to eight-year-olds. While they may recognize that their young children are using more of these newer digital technologies the majority of parents surveyed (57%) are not concerned about it. Video games are the technology most likely to be viewed negatively by the parents of young children (Wartella et al., 2013).

Second, smartphones and tablets are different from the more traditional audiovisual media of film and television, in that they are mobile. Children are no longer tethered to their home or a specific location to use smartphones or tablets. It is easy for parents and children to move around their house, their neighborhoods, their cars and in public spaces while using both smartphones and tablets. Indeed, we have become somewhat inured to watching pedestrians crossing streets while talking on their phones and with earbuds listening to music. Mobility brings with it the possibility of always being connected to the device and, indeed, the smartphone appears to have acquired that status with older youth and adults. There are few spaces that are technology-free zones − not in restaurants or schools or even somewhat in children's bedrooms. There is some evidence that calls to reduce children's access to screen media at bedtime (so as not to interrupt children's sleep).

This is understood by parents in that Rideout (2017) reports that only 29% of the parents of children under eight report allowing their children to have screen media in their bedrooms at night.

Third, both tablets and smartphones have multiple uses, which increases their attraction to children and adults. One can talk on the phone or watch videos or access the internet for a variety of information searches. Similarly, the tablet provides access to information, games, music and videos anytime and anywhere. The proliferation of apps with claims of providing children with educational content (more than 50,000 apps in the Apple Store call themselves educational) to teach them their letters, reading skills, literacy and math are widely available for children. This content can be tailored to the age and interests of the child. How different this is from the television era when only certain times in the broadcast week could parents find either educational programming or any age-appropriate children's programming. Even access to children's cable channels did not assure that the program being aired was appropriate for any aged child as the popularity of the teen programs on those channels demonstrate.

Last, unlike the more traditional mass media where a message is sent from the producer of the content to the users in a one-way transaction, the digital media of today are interactive. Children's interactions with the screens elicit a response. Games have characters and actions that are controlled by the children, questions presented in apps can be answered by the child and lead to other questions and other answers, and playing one video on YouTube can then send the child on to other videos determined by an algorithm that considers the child's past interests and interactions with the site. This ability for interaction is another attraction for young children. For the very young child who enjoys repetition of content these digital technologies can provide continuous repetition of content they enjoy.

"We may find that the affordances of smartphones and tablets are especially helpful learning tools for young children."

What are the implications of these features of smartphones and tablets? It seems to me that they are in very significant ways different from earlier media and technologies. These differences are especially attractive to very young children. All technologies have both benefits and potential risks. Consider, for instance, that these mobile technologies, easily used by young children, offer access to content that aids their development with learning opportunities. The early history of *Sesame Street* is illustrative of this point: *Sesame Street* when it went on the air in 1968 was intended for five-year-olds, to teach them their letters and numbers from one to 20. Over time we learned how much more preschoolers could learn under the right conditions and now *Sesame Street* teaches pre-reading skills (much beyond letter recognition) and a range of mathematical concepts. We may find that the affordances of smartphones and tablets are especially helpful learning tools for young children.

Ellen's Essentials

As for the risks involved? That is difficult to say, but we can raise some serious questions:

1. **What are the long-term consequences of early and heavy technology use from birth?**
2. **What sort of influence will such technology use have on developmental trajectories of, especially, social emotional development?**
3. **Will children's abilities to bond with peers, engage in meaningful face-to-face interactions change as a result of early and heavy media use?**
4. **What sorts of adults will today's technology-immersed children become?**
5. **What should we, as adults, do to ensure the healthy development of our children in this technologized world?**

References

AAP Council on Communications and Media. (2016). Media and young minds. *Pediatrics, 138*(5), 1–6.

Rideout, V. J. (2017). *The Common Sense Census: Media Use by Kids Age Zero to Eight.* San Francisco, CA: Common Sense Media.

Wartella, E., & Reeves, B. (1985). Historical trends in research on children and the media: 1900–1960. *Journal of Communication, 35*(2), 118–133.

Wartella, E., & Robb, M. (2008). Historical and recurring concerns about children's use of the mass media. In Calvert, S., & Wilson, B. (Eds.). *Handbook on Children and the Media* (pp. 7–26). Malden, MA: Blackwell Publishing.

Wartella, E., Rideout, V., Lauricella, A., & Connell, S. (Spring, 2013). *Parenting in the Age of Digital Technology: A National Survey.* Report for the Center on Media and Human Development School of Communication Northwestern University.

Learn More about Ellen's Work

Lauricella, A. R., Blackwell, C. K., & Wartella, E. (2017). The "new" technology environment: The role of content and context on learning and development from mobile media. In Barr, R., & Nichols Linebarger, D. (Eds.). *Media Exposure During Infancy and Early Childhood* (pp. 1–23). Switzerland: Springer International Publishing AG.

Wartella, E., Lauricella, A. R., Cingel, D., & Connell, S. (2016). Television, computers, and media viewing. In Friedman, H. (Ed.). *Encyclopedia of Mental Health*. Amsterdam, Netherlands, Elsevier/Academic Press.

Wartella, E., Beaudoin Ryan, L., Blackwell, C. K., Cingel, D. P., Hurwitz, L. B., & Lauricella, A. R. (2016). What kind of adults will our children become? The impact of growing up in a media-saturated world. *Journal of Children and Media*, *10*(1), 13–20. doi: 10.1080/17482798.2015.1124796

Lauricella, A. R., Wartella, E. A., & Rideout, V. J. (2015). Young children's screen time: The complex role of parent and child factors. *Journal of Applied Developmental Psychology*, *36*, 11–17.

Hurwitz, L. B., Lauricella, A. R., Hanson, A., Raden, A., & Wartella, E. (2015). Supporting Head Start parents: Impact of text message intervention on parent–child activity engagement. *Early Childhood Development and Care*, *185*(9), 1373–1389. doi: 10.1080/03004430.2014.996217

Ellen Recommends

Cole, C. (2016). *The Sesame Effect*. New York: Routledge.

Guernsey, L., & Levine, M. (2015). *Tap, Click, Read: Growing Readers in a World of Screens*. San Francisco, CA: Jossey-Bass.

Lemish, D., Jordan, A., & Rideout, V. (2017). *Children, Adolescents and the Media*. New York: Routledge.

Chapter 5

When the Technology Disappears

Lydia Plowman

In 1991, nearly 30 years ago, Michael Weiser wrote an article that appeared in *Scientific American* with the title 'The Computer for the 21st Century'. The article began with the words 'The most profound technologies are those that disappear. They weave themselves into the fabric of everyday life until they are indistinguishable from it' (1991).

He was way ahead of his time. During the 1990s a personal computer was typically a large, drab box connected to a power source with cables snaking between the monitor, the keyboard and the mouse. It was designed for adults to use in the workplace, not for children to use at home or in the kindergarten. Compare it with the smartphones and tablets that those of us living in wealthy economies have available to us now. The tethered desktop PC of the 1990s has almost been supplanted by these mobile devices that offer undreamed of connectivity and computational power. But, like the PC, they are still a single box – it's just that it fits in your pocket or purse.

Making predictions can be risky, but let's try some near-future gazing based on what we know already. We are now in the midst of a transition to *ambient* computing – a merging of our digital and physical worlds that leads to the disappearance of the boundaries between what is or is not some sort of computer. Computational devices will be everywhere and nowhere: they'll be ubiquitous in the world around us but we won't be aware of many of them and so they won't seem to exist.

The Internet of Things provides some present-day examples of this. It is certainly ubiquitous but, as its name suggests, it primarily connects objects, devices and gadgets – in other words, *things* that are visible. Although many of these things are familiar to us, they are not always what they seem because chips and sensors can be invisibly embedded in them. The concept of joining these things together is not completely unfamiliar as most of us understand that the internet connects billions of computing devices such as laptops and smartphones and that we can link our smartphones, tablets and work computers so that they can share files. Plus, there are many cases already where we're barely aware of computers. They control our heating systems, washing machines and microwave ovens – and, beyond the home, traffic systems, street lighting and pollution trackers.

"The most profound technologies are those that disappear. They weave themselves into the fabric of everyday life until they are indistinguishable from it." (Weiser, 1991, author's italics)

These internet connections are invisible, but once the things themselves are invisible too, our interactions with people, places and objects will change radically. As educators and parents, we should be thinking about the implications for digital play and learning when the technology is no longer clearly visible, because these changes are happening fast. Ambient computing has the potential to disrupt how we interpret and interact with our physical environment because it makes possible Weiser's long-predicted disappearance of the digital device. This is not just about its external visibility: he argues that it's only when people are no longer aware of using the device that it disappears. In order to achieve this, the means of interaction needs to be so intuitive and so close to natural forms of human communication that it doesn't require a specific language or movement of the hand to achieve its purpose. The information or service it provides – whether for work or play – needs to be so integral to our everyday goals and desires that it does not impose itself on us and so we don't notice it.

This is already beginning to happen: emerging forms of gesture, gaze and voice recognition fuelled by artificial intelligence and always-on connectivity mean that keyboards and track pads are becoming redundant. We are already beginning to see devices, such as virtual assistants, that use voice rather than a screen for the main form of interaction. So, screens, the means of input and the device itself could change out of all recognition.

Our practice as educators sometimes lags behind the pace of change – we see this now with children often exposed to more sophisticated technologies at home than in their early learning settings and the persistence of anxieties about screen time. Practice shouldn't be driven by technology, but educators can take an active role in ensuring that they and the children in their care benefit from these changes and the potential for adverse effects can be curbed. It may be difficult to envision the future as perceptively as Weiser, but we need to consider whether and how children's play and learning will change. Although he says that it's difficult to really give a sense of what it'll be like to live in a world full of what he calls 'invisible widgets', Weiser believes that the process of trying to think this through is worthwhile.

"Designing for young children in a world of ambient computing provides a wonderful opportunity to explore the ways in which technology can provide fun, pleasure and play."

Technology has been associated with concerns that the child's imagination and playfulness may diminish, but if the disappearing computer means that we can play with technology without needing to think about *how* to do just that, perhaps we can be freed up to become more imaginative and creative by exploiting the easier interactions and more playful behaviours that are made possible. Children's early years provide a test bed for designing in ways that might offer these possibilities. Designing for young children means that written text can't be the mechanism for providing instructions or input. This can be seen as a constraint, but it frees up designers to unleash their creativity. Designing for young children in a world of ambient computing provides a wonderful opportunity to explore the ways in which technology can provide fun, pleasure and play.

But it would be naïve to think that future changes will be universally welcomed. Weiser also had the far-sightedness to predict privacy as the key issue when connected computing devices that can sense presence and record conversations and actions are everywhere. The new generation of devices can collect data on a massive scale. But rather than using watch-like activity trackers or in-app logging of data at an individual level, this can be done invisibly and unobtrusively. This raises questions about the ways in which these technologies may shape children's behaviour, how the data generated by the devices from their activity is used and to what extent children, parents and educators are aware of, and can consent to, the technology's capabilities.

We have already seen an alert from the FBI about the privacy implications of data collected by some internet-connected toys. We may feel relaxed about collecting biometric data such as heart rate and body temperature that warns of undiagnosed medical conditions. But educators may not feel so positive about learning analytics applied to data from preschool children in ways that parallel the predictive modelling used to determine the performance of university students. Rather than the records of attendance, exams and online tests used to assess older students, ambient computing makes it possible to capture a much more diverse range of data. A child's movements, gestures, facial expressions, play patterns and attempts at reading or writing can generate data that's crunched to give educators on-the-fly information about a child's learning. Is this a risk or an opportunity? Some might see this as a useful opportunity for advance warning of developmental delays and learning difficulties; others might focus on the risk of branding a child as lacking in motivation or engagement at the age of three or four. The language of 'supporting' and 'improving' education and devising appropriate interventions may be more sinister than it first appears if children and their parents are not aware of the data being collected.

"A child's movements, gestures, facial expressions, play patterns and attempts at reading or writing can generate data that's crunched to give educators on-the-fly

information about a child's learning. Is this a risk or an opportunity?"

Perhaps this seems a bit sci-fi. Soothsayers have been predicting both utopian and dystopian technological futures for many years, but it looks as if Weiser's projection into the future was uncannily accurate. The disappearance of some of the technologies with which we're familiar will probably be both exciting and scary: innovative products that open up possibilities for new forms of interaction and recognize how young children learn, create and communicate could be beneficial but they could also compromise privacy and trust. So, this is a call to designers to heed the voices of children and educators by involving them in the co-creation of usable, playable products that meet children's cognitive, emotional and social needs. It's also a call to educators to do what they can to be aware of the emerging technologies around the corner and to find ways to ensure that they are safe, appropriate, playful and trustworthy.

Lydia's Essentials

1. **Children often have access to new products at home before they'll be in a preschool setting.** Being aware of what they play with at home and the potential uses in your own setting will enable you to keep on top of changes.
2. **Developing existing mechanisms to support links between home and preschool means that discussions with parents can systematically include children's experiences with home technologies in the same way that educators routinely engage parents in talk about their child's developing literacies or other changes in their learning.**
3. **Try to avoid being dazzled or intimidated by the whizz-bang nature of new products.** Be careful to check products' terms and conditions and understand the data usage policy: what information is collected when registering or logging on and who has access to this data?
4. **It's difficult to understand the ins and outs of ambient computing, so seek advice from those in the know, if needed.**
5. **Think about ways in which children can be introduced to some of the key concepts, such as how a toy can seem to know information about them or can 'talk' to them.**

References

Weiser, M. (1991). The computer for the 21st century. *Scientific American, 265*(3): 94–104.

Learn More about Lydia's Work

Plowman, L. (2016). Rethinking context: Digital technologies and children's everyday lives. *Children's Geographies, 14*(2): 190–202.

Plowman, L. (2016) Learning technology at home and preschool. Chapter 6 in N. Rushby & D. Surry, eds., *Wiley Handbook of Learning Technology*, pp. 96–112. Chichester, Sussex: John Wiley.

Plowman, L., Stephen, C. & McPake, J. (2010) *Growing Up with Technology: Young Children Learning in a Digital World*. London: Routledge.

Lydia Recommends

Marsh, J., Plowman, L., Yamada-Rice, D., Bishop, J., Lahmar, J. & Scott, F. (2018). Play and creativity in young children's use of apps. *British Journal of Educational Technology, 49*(5): 870–882.

Marsh, J., Plowman, L., Yamada-Rice, D. & Bishop, J. (2016). Digital play: A new classification. *Early Years, 36*(3): 242–253.

Weiser, M. (1991) The computer for the 21st century. *Scientific American, 265*(3): 94–104.

Chapter 6

Seeing Is Believing
Racial Diversity in Children's Media

Kevin A. Clark

It is said that "seeing is believing." Media (books, television, film, video games, etc.) shapes children's understanding of the world around them and helps them make sense of people, places and events in their lives. The frequency with which children see reflections of themselves and depictions of others communicates the importance and societal status of various groups of people. So, it's no wonder that frequent exposure to negative content, stereotypical and unbalanced representations cause African American children to feel less positive about themselves and their abilities (Martins & Harrison, 2012). When you pick up a book to read to your child, or your child selects a toy to play with, don't you want it to be a positive reflection of your child's race, gender and culture?

> **"Imagine what would happen if all children read books, saw television programs, watched movies and played games that presented positive portrayals of people who look like them."**

What if White children were exposed to varied positive images of Black, Latino, Asian and Indigenous people? With the increasing number of children of color in our country, this issue is increasingly important. It is essential that early on and throughout their social and intellectual development, all children are exposed to media that authentically portrays people of color. With the growing number of children of color in our country, this issue is increasingly important.

To achieve authenticity in portrayals, more people of color must be engaged as content creators. African American and Latino children consume almost four more hours of media per day than their White counterparts (Rideout, Foher, & Roberts, 2010). In contrast, the number of game designers who are of African American or Latino descent is only 2.5%. Across film, broadcast, cable and streaming, only 12.6% of the content is produced by non-White directors (Smith, Choueiti, & Pieper, 2016), and only 25% of children's books feature main characters of color (9% African American, 8%

Asian American/Pacific Islander, 6% Latino and 2% American Indian). For children's television in particular, because much of its content is derived from children's literature and books, it is important to include varied and authentic voices from people of color. As an example, of the 9% of children's books featuring African American characters, only 36% were written by African Americans (Horning, 2017). With content creators being predominately White, and media consumers being more heavily people of color, there is a "creator-consumer divide."

This divide doesn't exist because of audiences – they embrace on-screen diversity. A survey on diversity in Hollywood (Hunt, Ramon, & Tran, 2016) revealed that viewers preferred films and television shows with diverse casts. Films with casts of 21 to 30% diversity had the highest median worldwide box office receipts as well as the highest median return on investment (Hunt et al., 2018). In terms of scripted broadcasts, programs with 41 to 50% diverse cast members scored the highest ratings in Black and White households alike. On cable television, White and Latino viewers preferred casts with 31 to 40% diverse casts. While African American households preferred cable television shows with more than 50% diverse cast members (Hunt, Ramon, & Tran, 2016).

In the realm of film and television, racial diversity adds value. Diversity at all levels of the creative team enables content that is authentic and representative. People are often exposed to content that doesn't include or accurately portray people of color and in some cases is negative and demeaning based on their race and/or gender identification (Rideout, Scott, & Clark, 2016). These misrepresentations begin with media geared towards young children. Studies of television and movie depictions demonstrate the power of the media to influence the public's behaviors and attitudes by shaping, cultivating or reinforcing cultural meanings (Kirby, 2011; Nisbet & Dudo, 2010). Because of the overrepresentation of people of color as poor and criminal in the media, White people may become fearful and/or feel less empathy towards them. Studies show that media images have the greatest impact on perceptions when viewers have less real-world experience with the topic; in other words, the "media world" can be mistaken for the real world, unless audiences have sufficient personal experience to counteract its effects. Therefore, the real-world results of media misrepresentation may include everything from African Americans receiving less attention from doctors to harsher sentencing by judges, lower likelihood of being hired for a job or admitted to school, lower odds of getting loans and an increased likelihood of having a negative interaction with law enforcement (Opportunity Agenda, 2011).

People of color must become a more vital and influential part of creating, developing and distributing content in their own image and voice, to counteract frequent exposure to negative and distorted representations and facilitate positive change in how children of color see themselves and are seen by others. As technology and media companies are increasingly lining up to become content distributors, there are more opportunities to ensure a diverse cadre of creators at all organizational levels. There should be more diversity in producers, artists/illustrators, animators, writers and executives who could bring their expertise, perspective and experience to bear throughout the creation process. Because every person wants to see him or herself reflected in the media they consume, media organizations should strive to have the composition of their organizations reflect the audiences they serve.

"Diversity throughout a creative organization yields more authentic representations and portrayals, resulting in media that is more relevant and impactful."

For media organizations who say they are committed to racial diversity in their content development process, "seeing is believing."

Kevin's Essentials

1. Expose young people to diverse representations and media (books, television, film, games, etc.); beyond the same representations of Martin Luther King, Jr., Harriet Tubman, Cesar Chavez, etc.
2. Ask for suggestions from students, parents, colleagues.
3. Media companies and production houses need to diversify their organizations from the executive (decisionmakers) to the trades (creatives) level.
4. Look at diversity across your classroom library in addition to individual books and media products.
5. Use diverse media products all year and not just for holidays or designated times.

References

Horning, K. (2017). *Publishing statistics on children's books about people of color and first/native nations and by people of color and first/native nations authors and illustrators.* Madison, WI: Cooperative Children's Book Center, University of Wisconsin-Madison. Available at: https://ccbc.education.wisc.edu/books/pcstats.asp.

Hunt, D., Ramon, A., Tran, M., Sargent, A., & Roychoudhury, D. (2018). *Hollywood diversity report: Five years of progress and missed opportunities.* Los Angeles, CA: Ralph J. Bunche Center for African American Studies at University of California, Los Angeles (UCLA).

Hunt, D., Ramon, A., & Tran, M. (2016). *2016 Hollywood diversity report: Business as usual.* Los Angeles, CA: Ralph J. Bunche Center for African American Studies at University of California, Los Angeles (UCLA).

Kirby, D.A. (2011). *Lab coats in Hollywood: Science, scientists, and cinema.* Cambridge, MA: MIT Press.

Martins, N. & Harrison, K. (2012). Racial and gender differences in the relationship between children's television use and self-esteem: A longitudinal panel study. *Communication Research, 39*(3), 338–357.

Nisbet, M. & Dudo, A. (2010). *Science, entertainment, and education: A review of the literature.* Washington, DC: Report for the National Academy of Sciences.

Opportunity Agenda. (2011). *Opportunity for black men and boys: Public opinion, media depictions, and media consumption.* San Francisco, CA: Tides Center. Available at www.opensocietyfoundations.org/sites/default/files/opportunity-agenda-20111201.pdf.

Rideout, V., Scott, K., & Clark, K. (2016). *The digital lives of African American tweens, teens, and parents: Innovating and learning with technology.* Available at https://cgest.asu.edu/digitallives.

Rideout, V.J., Foher, U.G., & Roberts, D.F. (2010). *Generation M2: Media in the lives of 8- to 18-year-olds: A Kaiser family foundation study.* Menlo Park, CA. Available at https://kaiserfamilyfoundation.files.wordpress.com/2013/01/8010.pdf.

Smith, S.L., Choueiti, M., & Pieper, K. (2016). *Inclusion or invisibility? Comprehensive Annenberg report on diversity in entertainment.* Los Angeles, CA: Annenberg School of Communication and Journalism, University of Southern California.

Learn More about Kevin's Work

Clark, K. (2017). Practical applications of technology as a key to reducing the digital divide among African American youth. *Journal of Children and Media.* New York: Taylor & Francis Group.

Clark, K. (2016). Technology tools for family engagement: The role of diversity. In C. Donohue (Ed.), *Family engagement in the digital age: Early childhood educators as media mentors* (pp. 21–22). New York, NY: Routledge.

Rideout, V., Scott, K., & Clark, K. (2016). *The digital lives of African American tweens, teens, and parents: Innovating and learning with technology.* Available at https://cdmid.gmu.edu.

Clark, K. (2013). Diversity in children's media is more than just race or gender (Invited Blog Post). *The Fred Rogers Center.* Available at www.fredrogerscenter.org/blog/diversity-in-childrens-media-is-more-than-just-race-or-gender/.

Clark, K. & Sheridan, K. (2010). Game design through mentoring and collaboration. *Journal of Educational Multimedia and Hypermedia, 19*(2), 125–145.

Clark, K. (2008). Educational settings and the use of technology to promote the multicultural development of children. In G. Berry, M. Ellis, & J. Asamen (Eds.), *Handbook of child development, multiculturalism, and media* (pp. 411–418). Newbury Park, CA: Sage Publications.

Kevin Recommends

Annenberg Inclusion Initiative. (Stacey Smith, PhD) Available at https://annenberg.usc.edu/research/aii.

Berry, G.L. & Asamen, J.K. (1993). *Children & television: Images in a changing sociocultural world.* Newbury Park, CA: Sage Publications.

Diversity and Cultural Literacy Toolkit. Available at www.slj.com/?detailStory=diversity-cultural-literacy-toolkit.

Hollywood Diversity Report. (Darnell Hunt, PhD) Available at https://bunchecenter.ucla.edu/hollywood-diversity-report-2/.

Publishing statistics on children's books about people of color and first/native nations and by people of color and first/native nations authors and illustrators. Madison, WI: Cooperative Children's Book Center, University of Wisconsin-Madison. Available at http://ccbc.education.wisc.edu/books/pcstats.asp.

Chapter 7

Claiming Rights and Righting Wrongs

Children's Rights in the Digital Environment

Sonia Livingstone

Society's rapid adoption of digital technologies is reconfiguring the conditions and possibilities of childhood in the twenty-first century. Researchers are tracking the consequences for children's opportunities – to learn, communicate, play and connect, and for the associated risks of harm. These latter include the risks of exclusion from not being able to use the internet as much as more privileged others as well as the risks linked to using the internet – aggressive, sexual, privacy and identity risks, and new forms of surveillance and exploitation, among others. While governments, policymakers and educators are trying to grasp the significance of these digital transformations, so as to put in place appropriate, proportionate and effective strategies to support children (Livingstone, Carr & Byrne, 2015), parents and caregivers often find themselves at the sharp end, struggling to understand what's best for their child without much guidance or prior experience to call on (Livingstone & Sefton-Green, 2016).

All this is important, yet familiar, because we are all facing digital challenges in our personal as well as our professional lives. Every researcher and policymaker I meet is keen to tell me about their own child's experiences – whether with parental pride or a frown of anxiety. Less often heard is what diverse children around the world want for their digital present and future. On the one hand, they are enthusiastically embracing new technologies, keen to claim the latest innovations for themselves, creatively making them meaningful, proud of their digital expertise and hopeful for the digital future. But, on the other, they have concerns of their own about losing agency as they get caught up in complex digital services they cannot always understand or control. When asked in deliberative citizen juries, they also have lots of ideas about what should be done (Coleman, Pothong, Perez Vallejos & Koene, 2017).

But who is listening? It amazes me that a society ready to celebrate "digital natives" or worry about "digital addicts" is not much good at listening to children. If we do listen to them, the first thing they tell us is that they see access to digital technologies as their fundamental human right (Third et al., 2014). Don't take it away! Improve connectivity! It's our lifeline! We hear this not only for children from the world's wealthiest countries but also, strikingly, from its poorest – where complaints about problems with access are loudest and workarounds to connectivity are more creative (UNICEF, 2017).

Indeed, children increasingly see digital technologies – along with the digital literacy, agency and privacy to use them – as their preferred (and sometimes only) way to access their fundamental human rights across the board. What rights, you may ask? The UN Convention on the Rights of the Child sets out in a succinct yet inspirational document the full range of children's rights (UNCRC, 1989). It builds on international human rights frameworks (applicable to everyone, albeit often implicitly thought of as for adults – consider public discussion of the rights to freedom of expression, assembly or privacy). It also includes some rights especially for children (such as the rights to develop to one's full potential, to protection by parents or caregivers, to play and, recognizing that children's expression is routinely overlooked, to be heard in matters that affect them) (Lievens et al., 2018).

> **"Children increasingly see digital technologies – along with the digital literacy, agency and privacy to use them – as their preferred (and sometimes only) way to access their fundamental human rights across the board."**

Ratified by every country in the world except the USA, the Convention is the legal standard which obligates States to respect, protect and fulfil children's rights. This includes, it is being belatedly and somewhat reluctantly recognized, in relation to the digital environment. In its 2014 rallying cry to governments, and recognizing that "What happens offline today, will also be manifest online and what happens online has consequences offline," the UN Committee on the Rights of the Child demanded that: States should adopt a national coordinating framework with a clear mandate and sufficient authority to coordinate all activities related to children's rights and digital media and ICTs at cross-sectoral, national, regional and local levels and facilitate international cooperation.(OHCHR, 2014).

This was because, still, policy, legislative and regulatory mechanisms do not adequately support and protect children online. Many young internet users around the world do not have the benefit of appropriate forms of adult guidance from parents, teachers and other caregivers. The need for reliable, evidence-based mechanisms and guidance spans the full range of children's rights, but this is too often unrecognized, or little understood, in many countries. Such difficulties themselves tend to result in anxiety, impeding the search for proportionate, evidence-based, sustainable solutions and remedies that support children as independent rights-holders.

"The need for reliable, evidence-based mechanisms and guidance spans the full range of children's rights, but this is too often unrecognized, or little understood, in many countries."

Four specific challenges – of legal interpretation, policy implementation and effective enforcement – arise from the particular nature of the digital:

1. *Who is a child*, and the age and circumstances of a child, is often unknown and unknowable in the digital environment, with the digital environment largely designed, regulated and made accessible to a public implicitly conceived as adult (indeed, as a robust, digitally informed, able-bodied adult) (Livingstone & Third, 2017). This impedes decisions, policy and practice that respect the always-particular, necessarily contextual "best interests" of the child.

2. Real-world *disadvantages and vulnerabilities tend to be amplified* in the digital environment, necessitating protections, and yet the digital world can provide crucial support for children facing extreme difficulty. This intensification of children's protection and participation rights can generate conflict, with provision of opportunities inadvertently exposing children to risk, and with protective efforts so wrapping them in cotton wool that they can neither exercise their agency nor develop needed resilience (Livingstone, Haddon & Görzig, 2012).

3. *Parents are distinctively disempowered by the digital.* Although parents and caregivers are the traditional duty-bearers responsible for protecting and supporting children, it is difficult for governments to rely on parents as solely responsible for the child's well-being in relation to digital technology. The design of the digital environment tends to undermine the forms of parental oversight and consent that child protection has traditionally relied on offline, offering mainly clumsy, intrusive or widely ignored mechanisms (Livingstone, 2018).

4. *Online operations are fast-changing, opaque and complexly interdependent.* Businesses increasingly embed value decisions into their operations through use of automated algorithms which infer user characteristics to target marketing. The consequences – though potentially problematic in terms of consent, bias, discrimination, accuracy, accountability or even legality – are difficult to assess, especially given the huge power of some global companies (potentially infringing the child's rights to non-discrimination and privacy) (UN OHCHR, 2011).

To help governments navigate these challenges, in 2018 the Council of Europe adopted a formal Recommendation which sets out the principles to be followed, the standards to be met and the practicalities to be implemented to ensure that children's rights are fulfilled in the digital environment

(Council of Europe, 2018). It's a fairly short document, and if it were fully implemented, the prospects for children's well-being in the digital age would be hugely improved.

But it must be acknowledged that, in addition to challenges regarding the digital, there are also challenges linked to a child-rights-based approach. Here's four:

1. *Rights claims risk becoming righteous* – especially problematic when they brandish the authority of the United Nations to impose universalizing (or worse, Western-centric) assumptions in circumstances where local contexts and "voices from below" are not taken into account (Hanson, 2014). Examples include the One Laptop per Child project which air-lifted hardware into impoverished communities in the Global South with little attention to what teachers had been trained for or the fit with cultural expectations or local needs (Ames, in press). But poor implementation of children's rights to education and information doesn't make those rights wrong; it just means that properly consulta-tive, community-led implementation should be prioritized.

2. *Human rights are only called for in their absence.* If children were already able to explore and experiment online without coming to harm, there would be little call for a child-rights approach. So, the very focus on rights seems to belie their ineffectiveness, leaving them as an inspir-ational rallying cry at best, an ineffectual misdirection of effort at worst (Moyn, 2018). Yet, it matters that society has a way to codify and refer to the international consensus about what's important for children, informed by evidence and argumentation, so that it can be efficiently and effectively drawn upon when approaching the next challenge – in this case, the digital – without always having to start over.

3. *Rights frameworks don't help when rights clash.* As they do. It's all very well saying that rights should not be ranked, but this offers little guid-ance when the child's right to privacy clashes with the parent's effort to monitor them protectively. Or when children's participation rights – to meet new people online, say – clash with their right to be protected from strangers. What about when society doesn't agree on a child's rights – to sexual expression, for example. The only course of action here is to argue that a holistic approach is vital to balance relevant con-siderations in the best interests of the child. This helps ensure that policy and practice are adjusted to children's circumstances rather than blithely imposed on children as a category.

4. *Human rights concern the individual rights-bearer and are addressed to the State.* Arguably both are misplaced. To focus on the individual child may fit the neo-liberal rhetoric of our times (which favors individual choice and self-determination over the collective good), but it doesn't illuminate what's also needed in the digital environment: communal

learning resources, civil communities, collaborative networks for sharing creativity, public spaces for dialogue and action. Nor is easy to demand these when the digital infrastructure of our lives is increasingly proprietary, run to suit the commercial interests of global corporations who easily evade national jurisdiction. Yet States do have resources and mechanisms to address the individual and collective needs of their population; it is time to exercise these in relation to the digital environment, including for children.

So, what's the way forward? As the digital infrastructure on which society increasingly relies becomes ever more salient, often problematically (Plantin & Punathambekar, 2018), we oscillate between utopian and dystopian imaginaries, thereby intensifying calls for better regulation in the public interest. Yet, the more that high-level expertise and investment is directed towards possible solutions, the more children's rights risk being sidelined. So, let's end with two vital questions for critical scholarship:

- *How can children's voices be better heard?* By themselves listening to children, exploring their worlds or evaluating digital initiatives with their interests in mind, as well as insisting on meaningful forms of child participation in institutional procedures of all kinds, surely researchers and child-rights advocates can raise the profile of children's voices in policymaking and the development of new practice models.
- *How can children's rights in the digital environment be better addressed?* Article 29 of the UN Convention on the Rights of the Child asserts the importance of "the development of the child's personality, talents and mental and physical abilities to their fullest potential." While there will continue to be risks associated with a rights approach, if we keep asking of each new digital development how it could better support the development of children's fullest potential, and then act on the answer, we will at least be heading in a positive direction.

References

Ames, M. (in press). *The charisma machine: The life, death, and legacy of One Laptop per Child*. Cambridge, MA: MIT Press.

Coleman, S., Pothong, K., Perez Vallejos, E., & Koene, A. (2017). *Internet on our own terms: How children and young people deliberated about their digital rights*. Available at https://casma.wp.horizon.ac.uk/casma-projects/5rights-youth-juries/the-internet-on-our-own-terms/.

Council of Europe. (2018) *Recommendation CM/Rec(2018)7 of the Committee of Ministers to member States on Guidelines to respect, protect and fulfil the rights of the child in the digital environment*. Available at www.coe.int/en/web/children/-/new-recommendation-adopted-on-children-s-rights-in-the-digital-environment.

Hanson, K. (2014). "Killed by charity": Towards interdisciplinary children's rights studies. *Childhood, 21*(4): 441–446.

Lievens, E., Livingstone, S., McLaughlin, S., O'Neill, B., & Verdoodt, V. (2018). Children's rights and digital technologies. In T. Liefaard & U. Kilkelly (Eds.), *International children's rights law*, pp. 1–27. Berlin: Springer, doi:10.1007/978-981-10-3182-3_16-1.

Livingstone, S. (2018) The value of children's privacy in the regulation of personal data protection. *Intermedia, 46*(2): 18–23. Available at www.iicom.org/intermedia/inter media-past-issues/intermedia-july-2018/children-a-special-case-for-privacy.

Livingstone, S., Carr, J., & Byrne, J. (2015) *One in three: The task for global internet governance in addressing children's rights.* Global Commission on Internet Governance: Paper Series. London: CIGI and Chatham House. Available at www.cigionline.org/publi cations/one-three-internet-governance-and-childrens-rights.

Livingstone, S., Haddon, L., & Görzig, A. (Eds.). (2012). *Children, risk and safety online: Research and policy challenges in comparative perspective.* Bristol: Policy Press.

Livingstone, S., & Sefton-Green, J. (2016). *The class: Living and learning in the digital age.* New York: New York University Press.

Livingstone, S., & Third, A. (2017). Children and young people's rights in the digital age: An emerging agenda. *New Media & Society, 19*(5): 657–670. Available at http://eprints.lse.ac.uk/68759/.

Moyn, S. (2018). *Not enough: Human rights in an unequal world.* Cambridge, MA: Harvard University Press.

OHCHR. (2014). *Committee on the Rights of the Child: Report of the 2014 day of general discussion "digital media and children's rights".* Available at www.ohchr.org/Docu ments/HRBodies/CRC/Discussions/2014/DGD_report.pdf.

Plantin, J.-C., & Punathambekar, A. (2018). Digital media infrastructures: Pipes, platforms, and politics. *Media, Culture & Society.* ISSN 0163-4437. Available at http://eprints.lse.ac.uk/90876/.

Third, A., Bellerose, D., Dawkins, U., Keltie, E., & Pihl, K. (2014). *Children's rights in the digital age: A download from children around the world.* Melbourne, VIC: Young and Well Cooperative Research Centre. Available at www.westernsydney.edu.au/__data/assets/pdf_file/0003/753447/Childrens-rights-in-the-digital-age.pdf.

UN Office of the High Commissioner for Human Rights. (2011). *Guiding principles on business and human rights.* New York and Geneva: United Nations. Available at www.ohchr.org/Documents/Publications/GuidingPrinciplesBusinessHR_EN.pdf.

UNCRC (United Nations Convention on the Rights of the Child). (1989). Available at www.ohchr.org/Documents/ProfessionalInterest/crc.pdf.

UNICEF. (2017). *State of the world's children: Children in a digital world.* New York: UNICEF. Available at www.unicef.org/publications/index_101992.html.

Learn More about Sonia's Work

Livingstone, S. (2015) Children's digital rights. *Intermedia, 42*(4/5): 20–24. Available at http://eprints.lse.ac.uk/60727/ (4-page accessible article).

Sonia Livingstone talks to Giles Dilnot about digital rights for children. June 2017. Podcast (4 minutes). Available at https://soundcloud.com/user-607824267/sonia-living stone-talks-to-giles-dilnot

Livingstone, S., & Third, A. (2017) Children and young people's rights in the digital age: An emerging agenda. *New Media & Society*, *19*(5): 657–670. Available at http://eprints.lse.ac.uk/68759/

Sonia Recommends

Kidron et al. (2018) *Disrupted childhood: The cost of persuasive design*. London: 5Rights. Available at https://d1qmdf3vop2l07.cloudfront.net/eggplant-cherry.cloudvent.net/compressed/bb24215ada7264f0db4b3a0060e755b1.pdf

Third, A., Bellerose, D., Dawkins, U., Keltie, E., & Pihl, K. (2014). *Children's rights in the digital age: A download from children around the world*. Melbourne, VIC: Young and Well Cooperative Research Centre. Available at www.westernsydney.edu.au/__data/assets/pdf_file/0003/753447/Childrens-rights-in-the-digital-age.pdf

UNICEF. (2017). *State of the world's children: Children in a digital world*. New York: UNICEF. Available at www.unicef.org/publications/index_101993.html (includes several languages, and interactive and summary versions).

Chapter 8

Child-Centered Design
Integrating Children's Rights and Ethics into the Heart of the Design Process

Shuli Gilutz

The digital revolution has shaken up many industries – from TV to transportation, from telecommunications to music – and this is just the beginning. Children-related industries are trying to catch up, contemplating the design of new digital environments for kids that would complement, enhance, and sometimes replace, traditional media, toys, games, and learning activities. With changing business models, excitement for new technology capabilities, and wary yet enthusiastic response from parents, we have seen the rise of a plethora of new products for kids. However, when focusing on new tech and business models, these may neglect core principles of design for children, that are critical to their development and well-being. This essay looks at child-centered design principles: What are they? Why should we use them? Who should use them? The ten principles of the *Designing for Children's Guide* will be discussed, as part of the designing for children's rights initiative with UNICEF, as well as future work.

What do Fidget Spinners, *Sesame Street*, Rainbow Loom rubber bands, LEGO, and Wii Sports have in common? All are highly successful products for kids, designed specifically for children's fun, needs, interests, and well-being, and all became highly successful. In addition to being different kinds of media, differences between these products include cultural and educational assumptions, marketing strategies, and ongoing development: Some have already outdone their fifteen minutes of fame, while others are still leading the way, and setting standards in children's design.

Designing products for children has been a long-standing profession, from household objects, to toys and games, to learning and entertainment. When Swedish social theorist Ellen Key wrote her groundbreaking book *The Century of the Child* in 1900, she advocated a child-centered approach to education, play, and parenting, and is considered the first to define progressive thinking regarding the rights, development, and well-being of children as interest of utmost importance to all society (Macinai, 2016). The Museum of Modern Art in NYC dedicated their exhibition about 20th century design for children to her, and presented a curated overview of "individual and collective visions for the material world of children, from utopian dreams for the 'citizens of the future' to the dark realities of political conflict and exploitation" (MOMA, 2012).

In today's discussions about design for children, the issue of technology's role brings up many emotions. On one hand, parents want their children to enjoy the possibilities new technologies may afford them for play and learning, but on the other hand fears of changing social patterns, excessive screen time, and unknown consequences loom. In her book *Screen Time* (2012), contributing author Lisa Guernsey extensively reviews research about media and technology for young children aged zero to five and urges parents to shift from focusing on how much time their kids spend with screens, to what they are doing there, with whom, and what the alternatives are. Focusing on content, context, and the individual child, we can discover wonderful interactions that weren't possible without technology and omit others that may be hindering children's well-being (Guernsey, 2012).

The thing is, for children, this distinction is just weird. If you talk to children about technology, they will try to figure out what exactly you're referring to: The TV? Computer? Tablet? Microwave? Car? Walkie-talkie? Music player? And the list goes on. The distinction of "screens" and "internet connectivity" are technical ones made by adults who haven't grown up with these items, and therefore view them as novelty. For today's children, also known as Gen Z, real-time connectivity is taken for granted as their parents took for granted the presence of electricity. Children watch TV shows on their phone, play video games on TV, chat with their grandparents on their tablets, and order food with their family on the computer. These technologies are all tools, devices, to enhance their daily lives, and often they don't understand why adults fuss about them, especially since most adults use them drastically more often than children.

"The distinction of 'screens' and 'internet connectivity' are technical ones made by adults who haven't grown up with these items, and therefore view them as novelty."

Child-centered design refers to designing products for children by incorporating children's perspectives, needs, and rights, at the heart of the design process. It requires both (adult) designers and caregivers to deeply understand the children's world today, in order to create experiences for them that will enrich their lives, give them joy, and also prepare them for their future, as toys and play have always done.

Child-centered design derives from the User-Centered Design (UCD) approach, coined by Don Norman in the 1980s (Norman & Draper, 1986). To create highly usable and accessible products, the authors call to designers to empathize with the products' future users; understanding their needs, pain points, and delights, and incorporate the users themselves in the actual design process. When referring to child-centered design, this means that products that are well designed for children should be developed not only with true understanding of children's lives today, but also with children taking part in the design process. By not doing so companies end up basing their designs on myths and stereotypes, generational-gap fears and misunderstanding of children's perceptions.

The first unique difference when designing for kids is developmental differences. We have all been children, but that was a while ago, and in a different society. We watch the changes in childhood today, and want to combine both old and new, nostalgia and innovation.

While much has been discussed about today's kids as Digital Natives (Prensky, 2001), it is clear evolutional developmental changes don't occur over a couple of decades. The differences we see in children's abilities with technologies are mainly due to their early exposure to these devices and the improved accessible design. For example: A two-year-old can navigate You-Tube because the tablet's touch screen doesn't require the fine motor skills that a computer mouse required from kids a decade ago. That said, even one year of difference can be significant in how children comprehend and play. Designers must be keenly aware of the physical, cognitive, social, and emotional development of the children they are designing for.

The second main difference in child-centered design is the fact that children are minors. In the legal sense they have less responsibilities and rights than adults. In the commercial sense it means that they are not the customers, but the adults are. In 1989, the Convention on the Rights of the Child became the first legally binding international convention to affirm human rights for all children globally. UNICEF helps promote these rights to provision (health care, nutrition, education, and play), protection (from abuse, neglect, exploitation, and discrimination), and participation (participate in the decisions about their lives, communities, and services) (Convention of the Rights of the Child, 2018).

"Designers must be keenly aware of the physical, cognitive, social and emotional development of the children they are designing for."

Designing for children's rights means profoundly accepting and appreciating children's needs and applying a child-centered design process to create products that promote these ideas. This create products both children and parents love, but also promotes the notion that designing for children has great impact on society, from homes, to schools, to communities.

"You don't know me, so make sure to include me in the process."

In January 2018, a group of 70 designers, psychologists, and researchers gathered in Helsinki to create a *Children's Design Guide* based on children's rights (Children's Design Guide, 2018). Their work produced ten design guidelines for the best products for children, whether technology is involved or not, whether they are TV shows, podcasts, video games, apps, toys, or AI-based audio interactions. The guidelines are presented in a child's voice, to accentuate the core value of child-centered design.

1. *Right to Inclusion.* "I need a product that does not discriminate against gender, age, ability, language, ethnicity, culture and socio-economic status. I need to be able to enjoy it myself, and with my family, and friends."

2. *Right to Development.* "Give me control of play, learning, and tools, and offer support if I need it. Give me room to explore and support my growth."

3. *Right to Participation.* "Help me understand my place and value in the world. Involve me as a creator, contributor, not just a consumer."

4. *Right to Protection.* "Offer me something safe. Model safe behaviors and be my lifeguard when needed. Create designs that will allow me to easily know what is relevant to me, and what's not."

5. *Right to Privacy.* "Do not misuse my data. Help me keep control over my data by giving me choices about what data to share and let me know how my data is used. Do not take any more than you need, and do not monetize my personal data or give it to other people."

6. *Right to Leisure and Play.* "I am active, curious and creative but also like to chill. Allow for a variety of forms of play, as well as open-ended and child-led. Make it easy to set my own limits and help to develop and transform them as my understanding of the world around grows."

7. *Right to Community.* "Allow me to play with others: peers, family members, both close and far, Also, give me the opportunity to be independent and play on my own."

8. *Right to Information.* "Help me recognize and understand commer-cial activities. Make sure that I understand all relevant information that has an impact on me. This includes the terms and conditions of your product or service, in visuals, audio, and written text."

9. *Right to Healthy Life.* "Promote various activities and content that can help me live healthy; physical activities, connect with nature and my community, pique my curiosity for learning and exploring new ideas and content."

10. *Right to Be Heard.* "You don't know me, so make sure to include me in the process. You should spend time with me, my friends and my caregivers before you design a product or service. We have good

ideas that could help you. Also ensure that you talk with people who are experts on my needs."

There is no reason companies should compromise children's rights in designing for them, with excuses of cutting costs and making more profit. When looking at technology in the early years, products that adhere to these principles are ones that are both ethical and champion children's well-being. These will not only be the best products for kids, but also the ones parents and educators will trust. This, in turn, will help get the word out and expand the product's impact and reach to more children and communities.

Understanding the value of child-centered design, and designing for children's rights, is the beginning of making sense of the myriads of new technology (but not only) products for children. Like eco-friendly products, whose ethical and earth-friendly values are trumping low-cost non-sustainable toys, will child-centered design products create a baseline for quality products for children?

Shuli's Essentials

1. **Technology for children is not "good" or "bad."** It depends on the quality of content, the context of use, and the specific child's needs, interests, challenges, and passions.

2. **Trust children to develop a critical perspective about play, learning, and technology.** Discuss these issues with them and ask for their thoughts on pros/cons. You'll be surprised.

3. **When contemplating children's well-being, avoid nostalgia and generational gaps,** but rather look for children's rights and how those are embodied in new contexts.

4. **Allow for free play, with varying media and toys.** Observe social, cognitive, emotional, and physical play and learning, as kids' find their own ways to interact and have fun.

5. **Look for technology for children that addresses the design for children's rights guidelines.** Voice your opinions if products you use at school do not adhere to these principles and help get them motivated to improve their products and design ethically for kids.

References

Children's Design Guide. (2018). Retrieved from Children's Design Guide: https://chil drensdesignguide.org/.

Convention of the Rights of the Child. (2018, July 15). Retrieved from UNICEF: www. unicef.org/crc/.

Guernsey, L. (2012). *Screen Time: How Electronic Media – From Baby Videos to Educational Software – Affects Your Young Child.* New York: Basic Books.

Macinai, E. (2016). The century of the rights of children: Ellen Key's legacy towards a new childhood culture. *Journal of Theories and Research in Education, 11*(2), 67–76. doi:10.6092/issn.1970-2221/6375.

MOMA. (2012). *MOMA-Century of the Child*. Retrieved from moma.org: www.moma.org/interactives/exhibitions/2012/centuryofthechild/#/timeline/avant-garde-play time/.

Norman, D. A., & Draper, S. W. (1986). *User-Centered System Design: New Perspectives on Human-Computer Interaction*. Boca Raton, FL: CRC Press.

Prensky, M. (2001). Digital natives, Digital immigrants: Part 1. *On the Horizon, 9*(5), 1–6. doi:10.1108/10748120110424816.

Learn More about Shuli's Work

- What social responsibility do UX designers have when it comes to teens and tech addiction?: https://theblog.adobe.com/social-responsibil ity-ux-designers-comes-teens-tech-addiction/
- Virtual reality for kids: A UX perspective https://youtu.be/ Fr2_q2SrDNs?t=10m
- UX for kids: Designing for the next generation of play. An overview of digital-tangible and hybrid toys, and classification of three design trends: Cross-platform play, complementary platforms, and hybrid plat-forms: https://youtu.be/7qVCuzBj1gw
- Researchers and Designers convene to create *Design for Children's Guide*: https://www.unicef-irc.org/article/1746-researchers-and-design ers-convene-to-create-designing-for-children-guide.html
- *Children (Ages 3-12) on the Web*, 3rd edition, by Nielsen Norman group: https://www.nngroup.com/reports/children-on-the-web/

Shuli Recommends

- *Children's Design Guide*. (2018): https://childrensdesignguide.org/
- *Parenting for Digital Future* (blog): http://blogs.lse.ac.uk/ parenting4digitalfuture/
- *Free to Learn* by Peter Gray (2013).
- *Screenwise: Helping Kids Thrive (and Survive) in Their Digital World* by Devorah Heitner (2016).
- *Screen Time: How Electronic Media – From Baby Videos to Educational Software – Affects Your Young Child* by Lisa Guernsey (2012).
- *Convention of the Rights of the Child*, UNICEF. (2018, July 15): https:// www.unicef.org/crc/

Chapter 9

Digital Play

Susan Edwards

In this chapter I consider research and thinking regarding the concept of digital play. Digital play is a relatively new idea in early childhood education. When digital technologies first entered early childhood education settings, researchers and teachers focussed mostly on the extent to which using technologies was likely to be beneficial or harmful for young children (Cordes & Miller, 2000; Clements & Samara, 2003). As the digital age progressed and digital technologies became more domesticated in the lives of very young children, the debate shifted from if digital technologies should be used by young children, towards consideration of the most effective use of technology with children (e.g. Parette, Quesenberry & Blum, 2010). This shift encompassed thinking about how to integrate digital technologies in early childhood education settings where play is historically valued as enabling learning. Here, play is often considered a means of exploration – a hands-on activity and form of social interaction that helps children build knowledge about their world (Platz & Arellano, 2011). As researchers and teachers thought about how to most effectively integrate digital technologies with play-based learning the notion of digital play began to emerge in the literature.

One of the earliest uses of the term digital play was by Stephen Kline, Nick Dyer-Witheford and Greig de Peuter (2003) in their book *Digital Play: The Interaction of Technology, Culture, and Marketing*. They described digital play as the participation of people in a 'mediatized global marketplace' (p. 23). In this work, defining digital play was not about understanding play as a means of learning in early childhood education – more a way of understanding how digital technologies and popular culture were co-evolving to create a context for social engagement. Nonetheless, the work was significant for bringing together the idea that digital interactions by people might be viewed as a form of play. Other researchers associated more specifically with early childhood education used existing theories of play to explain young children's interactions with digital technologies. For example, Johnson and Christie (2009) drew on the work of play theorist Corrinne Hutt (1971) to explain that children needed opportunities to explore how technology worked. Later, Bird and Edwards (2015) integrated Hutt's (1966) ideas about exploratory and symbolic play with Vygotsky's thinking regarding tool mediation. Vygotsky believed that as people mastered different tools they could use them in new ways. Bird and Edwards (2015) suggested that children used exploratory play to master technology as a tool and that this could lead to the use of digital technology as symbolic play. Verenikina and Kervin (2011) used the work of Singer and Singer (2006), Piaget (1952) and Vygotsky (1967) to describe children's digital play using iPads. Fleer (2016) also used Vygotsky's (1994) thinking to describe digital technologies as a pivot for children's symbolic thinking. Marsh et al. (2016) developed a typology of digital play based on the play-types identified by Bob Hughes and identified 'transgressive play' as a new form of digital activity for children.

In my own work, I argued for a contextual perspective in which digital play was viewed as a mode of meaning-making for young children responding to life in which digital technologies were used for communication, entertainment and participation within consumer-orientated societies (Edwards, 2013). I suggested that current approaches to digital technology provision in early childhood education were characterized in international curriculum frameworks by the separation of digital technologies from the use of play as a means of learning. By viewing young children's play as a form of meaning-making within digital contexts I was interested in how children and teachers could actively engage in problem-solving and critical thinking with and about digital technologies relative to children's play interests. At the time, I proposed a parallel movement in early childhood education based on the field of New Literacies Studies (The New London Group, 1996; Lankshear & Knobel, 2003; Kalantzis & Cope, 2012), in which context is understood to inform meaning-making for children and vice versa. In later work, this reference to the New Literacies Studies was further developed as a pedagogical movement towards New Play – the understanding that young children's engagement with digital technologies and digital media is always multimodal, involving children in locally experienced and yet global-level popular-culture digital technology interests, via the seamless integration of traditional and digital activities (Edwards et al., 2019).

> **"By viewing young children's play as a form of meaning-making within digital contexts I was interested in how children and teachers could actively engage in problem-solving and critical thinking with and about digital technologies relative to children's play interests."**

While I still understand context to be central to young children's meaning-making through play, in recent times I have been grappling with the extent to which a definition of digital play is going to be possible for the field. As Fleer (2016) noted in a recent socio-cultural explanation for digital play, the early childhood education sector has never entirely been able to settle on a definition of play itself. Some people view play as a developmental process, others as a form of engagement in socio-cultural contexts (Bergen, 2014). Play is also understood in terms of gender and power relationships amongst children (Grieshaber & McArdle, 2010), and is known to be culturally relative (Gaskins, 2014). Research similarly contests the extent to which play – as freely chosen by children, or mediated for learning by teachers, effectively enables learning in early childhood education settings (Pyle, DeLuca & Danniels, 2017). With these concerns regarding play alone generating pedagogical issues for the field, how might a useful definition of digital play be reached?

The 'digital' itself is not one thing. Should researchers and teachers consider 'digital' the actual technologies used by young children? Or is 'digital' about the capacity of technologies to process, store and retrieve data in digital form? Conversely, 'digital' will not be the same for all children in all places. Some children have more access to digital technologies than others. Research also shows that digital practices in childhood shape opportunities for later employment (Warschauer & Matuchniak, 2010). Productive digital practices, such as using technologies to create content, communicate with other people and share ideas are experienced more often by children in socially advantaged homes (Schradie, 2011). Children in less advantaged settings tend to use digital technologies for the consumption of content (Judge, Puckett & Bell, 2006). Arguably, access to digital technologies and modes of learning for using digital technologies for cultural participation is a matter of social equity. This means I also need to think about the 'digital' in terms of young children's life opportunities.

In my attempt to think about what these different aspects of the 'digital' might mean for a definition of digital play I have engaged in some wide-ranging reading. I have considered the technical history of the digital age – beginning with Einstein's ideas about matter and how this enabled the eventual invention of the transistor, leading to the microprocessor as the base unit for digitizing data (see, for example: Stephen & Edwards, 2017). I have also spent time reading the Philosophy of Technology (Gibbons, 2010), a body of knowledge that seeks to understand the relationship between people, society and technology. Within this body of work, it is Andrew Feenberg's (1991) idea regarding critical theory of technology that I consider most interesting for early childhood education regarding the notion of digital play. Feenberg suggests that technologies are always created and used according to human values. He has a concept called the 'technical code' (Feenberg, 2005) that explains how human values become integrated with technologies. A technical code occurs when people begin to use technologies in accordance with what they already value or consider important within their community of practice. These values begin to shape what and how technology is used in practice. Eventually, the technology is used in line with the practices associated with the value, and not necessarily by the affordances of the technology itself.

In early childhood education, play is historically understood as a means of learning for young children. As researchers have attempted to integrate digital technologies into play-based learning, it is play that has come to be used as an informing value for digital technology use with young children – thus the concept of digital play. I believe that the research effort invested in understanding digital play to date has been necessary for the sector. Digital play has allowed researchers and teachers to think about digital technologies in relation to children's play as meaning-making instead of separating technologies from play. This has been an important first step in understanding the integration of digital technologies in early childhood education. However, now that the field is actively debating, researching and teaching with the concept of digital play (Edwards, 2015; Arnott, 2016; Fleer, 2016; Marsh et al., 2016), I wonder about the sustainability of this concept as the digital age progresses. Already, children are using the Internet of Toys, wearable technologies are becoming more common and artificial intelligence, voice-activated technologies and big data are part of life. Here, it is the digital that matters for children as much as play.

Using Feenberg's (2005) logic, digital play may be viewed as technical code in which play shapes the use of digital technologies by teachers with children. Feenberg (2005) argues that one of the problems with a technical code is that the value inscribed on the technology informs how the technology is used within a given community even as the technological situation around people is evolving. Personally, I believe digital play suggests two issues that will require attention in the coming decades. First, digital play, whereby play reinscribes its value on the digital may bound the capacity of the sector to generate new professional knowledge about teaching and learning in the digital age in favor of increased thinking about play. However, Philosophy of Technology as a body of knowledge, including the critical work of Feenberg, technological determinist perspectives and substantive theory of technology, offers viewpoints on the relationship between people, technology and society that teachers could draw on as complementary informants to play as pedagogy (Gibbons, 2015). This suggests an expansion of the traditional knowledge base on which the sector draws to inform decision-making about learning in the digital age.

Second, and perhaps more importantly, play itself has known pedagogical issues in early childhood education. For example, research shows that not all young children learn through play and that learning through observation and direct teaching matters for children from diverse cultures (e.g. Gaskins, 2014). Also, the issue of how to balance open-ended play with intentional teaching for learning continues to manifest within the sector against pressures for increased learning outcomes in the early years (Pyle, DeLuca & Danniels, 2017). Digital play as a technical code suggests practices in digital technology provision that continue to value play as learning. At first glance this is not too concerning. However, for children coming from homes where digital technology use is associated with consumption rather than productive purposes, the value of digital play may not be entirely useful in learning how to use digital technologies for cultural participation. Some children, through no fault of their own, may experience a form of double digital disadvantage, first at home through patterns of technology use that promote digital consumption, and again in their early childhood education settings through a version of digital play as learning that fails to address cultural diversity and/or the role of intentional teaching in the acquisition of productive digital practices.

"Thinking about the digital as well as the play."

So where does all of this leave digital play? Digital play remains important for the early childhood education sector. It is still play to which the Western European early childhood education sector largely orientates for understanding learning; and so digital play itself does provide a familiar starting point for teachers regarding technology integration. However, I also believe that as research has worked so hard to establish a critical perspective on play as pedagogy, so too should this level of thinking now be directed towards understanding the 'digital' as it relates to young children's lives and learning. For me, asking if digital play is a technical code provides a starting point for this very process. To do otherwise is to neglect consideration of what a contextual perspective on digital play entails anyway – thinking about the digital as well as the play.

Susan's Essentials

1. Discuss with colleagues what you think digital play means.
2. Invite children and families to document and share their most frequently used digital technologies.
3. Research with children the origins of their most frequently used digital technologies.
4. Explore children's thinking about the future of digital technologies.
5. Identify the digital technology experiences you offer in your classroom that promote opportunities for children to build productive digital practices.

References

Arnott, L. (2016) An ecological exploration of young children's digital play: Framing young children's social experiences with technologies in early childhood. *Early Years*, *36*(3), 271–288.

Bergen, D. (2014). Foundations of play theory. In In L. Brooker., M. Blaise, & S. Edwards (Eds.), *SAGE handbook of play and learning in early childhood* (pp. 9–20). London: SAGE.

Bird, J., & Edwards, S. (2015). Children learning to use technologies through play: A digital play framework. *British Journal of Educational Technology*, *46*(6), 1149–1160.

Clements, D., & Samara, J. (2003). Strip mining for gold: Research and policy in educational technology – Response to fool's gold. *Association for the Advancement of Computing in Education Journal*, *11*(1), 7–69.

Cordes, C., & Miller, E., (2000). *Fool's gold: A critical look at computers in childhood*. College Park, MD: Alliance for Childhood.

Edwards, S. (2013). Digital play in the early years: A contextual response to the problem of integrating digital technologies and play-based learning in the early childhood curriculum. *European Early Childhood Education Research Journal*, *21*(2), 199–212.

Edwards, S. (2015). New concepts of play and the problem of technology, digital media and popular-culture integration with play-based learning in early childhood education. *Technology, Pedagogy and Education*, *25*(4), 513–532.

Edwards, S., Nuttall., J., Grieshaber, S., & Wood, E. (2019). New play: A pedagogical movement for early childhood education. In D. Whitebread (Ed.), with V. Grau, K. Kumpulainen, M. McClelland, D. Pino-Pasternak, & N. Perry, *The sage handbook of developmental psychology and early childhood education* (pp. 272–285). London: SAGE.

Feenberg, A. (1991). *Critical theory of technology* (Vol. 5). New York: Oxford University Press.

Feenberg, A. (2005). Critical theory of technology: An overview. *Tailoring Biotechnologies*, *1*(1), 47–64.

Fleer, M. (2016). Theorising digital play: A cultural-historical conceptualisation of children's engagement in imaginary digital situations. *International Research in Early Childhood Education*, *7*(2), 75–90.

Gaskins, S. (2014). Children's play as cultural activity. In E. Booker, M. Blaise, & S. Edwards (Eds.), *The Sage handbook of play and learning in early childhood* (pp. 31–42). London: Sage.

Gibbons, A. (2010). Reflections concerning technology: A case for the philosophy of technology. In S. Izumi-Taylor & S. Black (Eds.), *Technology for early childhood education and socialisation: Developmental applications and methodologies* (pp. 1–19). Hershey, NY: IGI Global.

Gibbons, A. (2015) Debating digital childhoods: Questions concerning technologies, economies and determinisms. *Open Review of Educational Research*, *2*(1), 118–127.

Grieshaber, S., & McArdle, F. (2010). *The trouble with play*. London: McGraw-Hill Education (UK).

Hutt, C. (1966). *Exploration and play in children*. Paper presented at the Symposia of the Zoological Society of London, London, England.

Hutt, C. (1971). Exploration and play in children. In R. Herron & B. Sutton-Smith (Eds.), *Child's play* (pp. 231–251). New York: Wiley.

Johnson, J. E., & Christie, J. F. (2009). Play and digital media. *Computers in the Schools*, *26*(4), 284–289.

Judge, S., Puckett, K., & Bell, S. M. (2006). Closing the digital divide: Update from the early childhood longitudinal study. *The Journal of Educational Research*, *100*(1), 52–60.

Kalantzis, M., & Cope, B. (2012). *New learning: Elements of a science of education*. Cambridge: Cambridge University Press.

Kline, S., Dyer-Witheford, N., & de Peuter, G. (2003). *Digital play: The interaction of technology, culture, and marketing*. Montreal, Quebec: McGill-Queen's Press-MQUP.

Lankshear, C., & Knobel, M. (2003). New technologies in early childhood literacy research: A review of research. *Journal of Early Childhood Literacy, 3*(1), 59–82.

Marsh, J., Plowman, L., Yamada-Rice, D., Bishop, J., & Scott, F. (2016) Digital play: A new classification. *Early Years, 36*(3), 242–253.

Parette, H., Quesenberry, A., & Blum, C. (2010). Missing the boat with technology usage in early childhood settings: A 21st century view of developmentally appropriate practice. *Early Childhood Education Journal, 37*(5), 335–343.

Piaget, J. (1952). *Play, dreams and imitation in childhood*. New York: Norton Library.

Platz, D., & Arellano, J. (2011). Time tested early childhood theories and practices. *Education, 132*(1), 54–63.

Pyle, A., DeLuca, C., & Danniels, E. (2017). A scoping review of research on play-based pedagogies in kindergarten education. *Review of Education, 5*(3), 311–351.

Schradie, J. (2011). The digital production gap: The digital divide and Web 2.0 collide. *Poetics, 39*(2), 145–168.

Singer, J., & Singer, D. (2006). Preschoolers' imaginative play as precursor of narrative consciousness. *Imagination, Cognition and Personality, 25*(2), 97–117.

Stephen, C., & Edwards, S. (2017). *Young children playing and learning in a digital age: A cultural and critical perspective*. New York: Routledge.

The New London Group. (1996). A pedagogy of multiliteracies: Designing social futures. *Harvard Educational Review, 66*(1), 60–93.

Verenikina, I., & Kervin, L. (2011). iPads, digital play and pre-schoolers. *He Kupu, 2*(5), 4–19.

Vygotsky, L. S. (1967). Play and its role in the mental development of the child. *Soviet Psychology, 5*(3), 6–18.

Vygotsky, L. S. (1994). The problem of the environment. In R. van der Veer & J. Valsiner (Eds.), *The Vygotsky reader* (pp. 338–354). Oxford, United Kingdom: Blackwell.

Warschauer, M., & Matuchniak, T. (2010). New technology and digital worlds: Analyzing evidence of equity in access, use, and outcomes. *Review of Research in Education, 34*(1), 179–225.

Learn More about Susan's Work

Beyond Screen Time webinar (Parenting Research Centre) www.youtube.com/watch?v=By6i2aOvE3w&feature=youtu.be

Stephen, C., & Edwards, S. (2017). *Young children playing and learning in a digital age: A cultural and critical perspective*. New York: Routledge.

Edwards, S. (2013). Digital play in the early years: A contextual response to the problem of integrating technologies and play-based pedagogies in the early childhood curriculum. *European Early Childhood Education Research Journal, 21*(2), 199–212.

Edwards, S., Straker, L., & Oakely, H. (2018). Early Childhood Australian statement on young children and digital technologies. www.earlychildhoodaustralia.org.au/wp-content/uploads/2018/10/Digital-policy-statement.pdf

Early Childhood Futures research www.facebook.com/LSIAECF/

Susan Recommends

Gibbons, A. (2015) Debating digital childhoods: Questions concerning technologies, economies and determinisms. *Open Review of Educational Research*, 2(1), 118–127.

Feenberg, A. (1991). *Critical theory of technology* (Vol. 5). New York: Oxford University Press.

Plowman, L. (2016). Rethinking context: Digital technologies and children's everyday lives. *Children's Geographies*, *14*(2), 190–202.

Warschauer, M., & Matuchniak, T. (2010). New technology and digital worlds: Analyzing evidence of equity in access, use, and outcomes. *Review of Research in Education*, *34*(1), 179–225.

The New London Group. (1996). A pedagogy of multiliteracies: Designing social futures. *Harvard Educational Review*, *66*(1), 60–93.

Chapter 10

Coding as Another Language

Why Computer Science in Early Childhood Should Not Be STEM

Marina Umaschi Bers

What does computer science have to offer us in the 21st century? From smart watches to cell phones to automated cars, most of our objects have been programmed. They demand some basic understanding of cause and effect, the ability to sequence actions to achieve our goals, and the disposition to problem solve when things do not work as expected. Furthermore, algorithms dictate the news displayed in our social media, the people we might enjoy meeting and the merchandise we might want to purchase. If we do not understand what an algorithm is, we might not understand why and how certain information is or is not presented to us.

While we, as consumers of new technologies, need a basic skillset to exert some control over the smart artifacts in our lives, those of us who might become producers of these technologies, need more sophisticated engineering and computer science knowledge. However, all of us, consumers and producers, need to learn how to think in new ways about issues we have never encountered before. That is the true power of learning computer science: developing new ways of thinking about ourselves and our world.

Although most of us can identify the act of thinking and recognize its value, there is no scholarly consensus on its definition. What is thinking? It is the ability to make sense, interpret, represent, model, predict and invent our experiences in the world. It is facilitated by language. As Vygotsky wrote: "Thought development is determined by language, i.e., by the linguistic tools of thought" (Vygotsky, 2012, p. 100). Thus, as educators, we must give children one of the most powerful tools for thinking: language.

This is clearly understood in early childhood education. There is a strong focus on both building language skills and on helping children transition from oral language to written language. The teaching of literacy has occupied the field for a very long time (National Early Literacy Panel, 2008). Today, we have the opportunity to not only teach children how to think by using natural languages, but also by learning artificial languages – programming languages. Those are the languages understood by the smart objects and the algorithms that surround us.

I am using the term "language" to refer to a system of communication, natural or artificial, composed of a formal system of signs, governed by syntactic and grammatical combinatory rules, that serves to communicate meaning by encoding and decoding information. These systems of signs can be, for example, spoken, textual, graphical, gestural or tangible. This broad definition encompasses natural languages such as English, Spanish or Japanese, computer languages such as C or ScratchJr, sign language and tangible languages such as KIBO robotics. All of these have in common a limited set of signs that represent meaning and that can be combined in multiple ways following a specific set of rules to convey meaning.

The achievement of literacy with a natural language involves a progression of skills beginning with the ability to understand spoken words, followed by the capacity to code and decode written words, and culminating in the deep understanding, interpretation and production of text. The ultimate goal of literacy is not only for children to master the syntax and grammar, the orthography and morphology, but also the semantics and pragmatics, the meanings and uses of words, sentences and genres. A literate person knows that reading and writing are tools for meaning making and, ultimately, tools of power because they support new ways of thinking. In this paper, I am proposing that teaching coding ought to resemble the educational process used for teaching literacy. However, in current times, when most efforts to introduce coding take advantage of the growing push for STEM (Science, Technology, Engineering and Math) education, the powerful linkage with literacy and language gets lost.

"A literate person knows that reading and writing are tools for meaning making and, ultimately, tools of power because they support new ways of thinking."

The Problem with STEM

In the United States, the STEM acronym began to be used in education to address the perceived lack of qualified candidates for high-tech jobs. STEM came into the American consciousness in the 1950s to train the workforce and maintain national security. In 1958, during the height of the Space Race, the United States passed the National Defense Education Act, which provided funding and incentives for schools to improve both STEM and modern foreign language curricula (Kuenzi, 2008). Throughout different historical periods, the acronym went through variations in the order of its letters, such as SMET and MSTE, but finally settled as STEM.

As the cold war ended, the emphasis on national security diminished and the urgency to teach a foreign language dropped, while the need for a technically savvy workforce grew. In 2015, the STEM Education Act was passed, the first time that federal funding for STEM was extended to cover computer science programs (Guzdial & Morrison, 2016). At the same time, well-funded nonprofits such as Code.org championed awareness and access to computer science in schools, by launching curricular initiatives, K-12 educational frameworks, professional development and policy changes.

The consolidation of STEM as a disciplinary cluster to fulfill the needs of the growing automated economy eclipsed the potential educational benefits of linking natural and artificial languages. As a result, schools isolated computer programming disciplinarily. It became the exclusive asset of STEM. However, things could have turned out differently. For example, what if instead of linking computer programming to economic growth and workforce preparation, it had been linked to intellectual growth and literacy education? What if the early argument had been that coding is about language? What if the pedagogies for teaching coding had borrowed teaching methods from literacy instead of math? What if the goal of teaching coding had been self-expression and communication, as opposed to problem-solving? Would this have allowed for a larger adult population that uses coding as a tool for creative expression and innovation and not just formulaic code writing? Would this have prevented the current lack of women and underrepresented minorities in the field? Would the cluster of STEM disciplines still own computer science? What if the role of computer science was conceived, from the beginning, not as a tool to educate the future workforce, but as a tool for thinking for the future citizenry? Throughout almost two decades, I have been pondering on these issues and developing technologies and pedagogical approaches to address the potential of teaching "Coding as Another Language" (CAL).

Coding as Another Language

Back in 1987, my mentor Seymour Papert called for the development of a field of study, which he called "computer criticism," by analogy with literary criticism. He wrote, "The name does not imply that such writing would condemn computers any more than literary criticism condemns literature ... The purpose of computer criticism is not to condemn but to understand, to explicate, to place in perspective" (Papert, 1987, p. 2). Papert envisioned that this new discipline would illuminate the role of computer programming in society and, most specifically, in education. Unfortunately, "computer criticism" never developed into a scholarly discipline, and the potential debate ended quickly by linking computer programming to STEM disciplines, instead of language arts or foreign languages. However, Papert and colleagues suggested that the process of learning to program may be akin to learning a foreign language in that they involve similar cognitive processes (Papert, 1980).

Although empirical research did not validate this observation, extensive work was done to design computational tools that reinforce the learning of

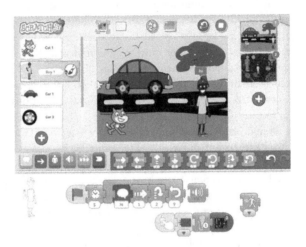

Photo 10.1 ScratchJr interface
Photo credit to Marina Umaschi Bers

Photo 10.2 KIBO robotic kit
Photo credit to Marina Umaschi Bers

coding as a literacy. For example, the DevTech Research Group that I direct at Tufts University has created programming environments for early childhood education, such as the free ScratchJr app (in collaboration with Mitch

Resnick at the MIT Media Lab) (see Photo 10.1) and the KIBO robotic system that uses tangible blocks instead of screens (see Photo 10.2), which teach coding with a literacy approach (Bers, 2018). In addition, our curricula, teaching materials and professional development strategies explicitly highlight the connection between the activity of coding and the mastering of a language and its uses to convey meaning. For example, in our *Dances around the World* curriculum, children learn to program their KIBO robots to dance to the beat of a culturally based traditional song and, at the end of the unit, invite family and friends to a robotic performance. While in the process of programming they learn powerful ideas from computer science and engineering, they engage in all steps of the design process, they put together their algorithms with the wooden KIBO command blocks and they debug their programs when things do not work, one of the most important activities they are doing is learning how to use a language to represent an idea and communicate something that is personally meaningful to them. I coined the term "Coding as Another Language" (CAL) to refer to our pedagogical approach.

CAL proposes that programming, as a literacy, engages new ways of thinking and new ways of communicating and expressing ideas – not only new ways of problem-solving. At a time when the US, among other nations, is struggling to understand if, how and when the teaching of computer science becomes mandatory, it is important to grapple with these pedagogical questions before policies are put in place. CAL understands programming languages as tools for thinking, and therefore, within this approach, learning to program as akin to learning how to use language.

A strong body of research in literacy education has helped us understand how young children learn to read and write and what instructional practices are most successful. Like any field of study there are dissenting camps, mostly rooted in differing beliefs about how literacy develops. Most famously, in the early 1990s, this debate led to the Reading Wars between proponents of a phonics emphasis in reading (cognitive theory) and proponents of whole language (maturation theory). But with increasing consensus, literacy scholars have embraced a "balanced diet" approach that agrees on the need for explicit phonic, phoneme and alphabetic strategy instruction, as well as authentic text and text-rich environments where discussion is central and student interpretations matter. Current understandings of literacy development provide a road map for how to transition students from oral language to written language through a series of fairly predictable stages (Chall, 1983; Duke & Pearson, 2002; Goldenberg, 1992). The assumption is that literacy is not a natural process like speech, where it unfolds in a child given the right conditions, but that it needs appropriate instruction, curriculum and assessment (Goldenberg, 2013). The same is true with coding.

Although the learning progressions for coding have not yet been as clearly identified as in literacy, work at my DevTech Research Group has contributed to describing the powerful ideas and skills in the continuum from proto-programmers to expert programmers in early childhood (Bers, 2018). As with literacy, the coding progression does not just happen naturally; it requires instructional strategies. CAL understands the process of coding as a semiotic act, a meaning making activity, and not only a problem-solving challenge, even during its earliest, most basic levels of instruction. This understanding shapes how we develop our curriculum and our strategies for teaching coding.

The field of computer science education in early childhood has not yet had its Coding Wars, and yet there are two sides competing for attention. On the one side, there are those who provide introductory coding experiences through challenges to be solved with limited tools and languages. For example, Code.org popularized structured puzzle-like challenges for problem-solving tasks. Most of their lessons in the K-2 sequence feature a series of increasingly complex mazes that vary in theme but essentially rely on direction cues to move an object around the screen. From a cognitive perspective, there is sequencing and problem-solving, but this approach deprives children of the most powerful impact of literacy: expression of their own voices through the making of meaningful artifacts. This is the hallmark of the other side: those of us who align our work with Papert's Constructionism (1980) and who believe in immersing young children in computer programming languages, such as ScratchJr and KIBO, which are developmentally appropriate and, at the same time, provide opportunities for creating personally meaningful computational projects. Through this process, children learn to both code and use the code as a language for expression (Bers, 2018).

"From a cognitive perspective, there is sequencing and problem-solving, but this approach deprives children of the most powerful impact of literacy: expression of their own voices through the making of meaningful artifacts."

This process is akin to moving from "learning to read" to "reading to learn" (Carnine & Carnine, 2004; Chall, 1983). CAL integrates the teaching of coding with all of the early childhood curriculum, not only STEM. Children who learn to code can apply those thinking skills, abstraction, logic and problem-solving to everything else. Researchers in computer science education have coined the term "computational thinking" to refer to universally applicable attitudes and skillsets, rooted in computer science, that are fundamental for everyone to master (Wing, 2006, 2011). Coding engages and reinforces computational thinking. At the same time, computational thinking engages and reinforces coding. However, CAL proposes that when coding is introduced, thinking must also promote personal expression, communication and interpretation, and not only problem-solving.

"As more people learn to code and computer programming leaves the exclusive domain of computer science to

become integral to other professions, it is more important than ever that we develop computer science pedagogies that promote deep and thorough engagement for everyone."

Understanding computer science as a component of STEM education has restricted the power of coding to a limited group of disciplines, to a limited group of students and teachers and to the particular demands of the workforce. It diminishes coding's power as a true literacy that promotes new ways of thinking. If education aims at helping people think creatively to solve the problems of our world, only a subset of those problems can be solved by STEM disciplines. As more people learn to code and computer programming leaves the exclusive domain of computer science to become integral to other professions, it is more important than ever that we develop computer science pedagogies that promote deep and thorough engagement for everyone.

The field of literacy research has demanded that literacy instruction go beyond the important but insufficient benchmark of mechanical decoding and comprehension and should teach our children how to *use* their reading and writing as a tool for expression. CAL now moves the goalpost for computer science education. Our call is simple: let's teach coding to our children in a way that exposes it for what it is, a new language. Through this approach, the civic dimension of literacy comes into play. We are leaving the scribal age, when literacy was limited to a few chosen ones, and entering the printing press era, when it is available for the masses. As a literacy of the 21st century, coding has the power to bring about social change.

Marina's Essentials

The CAL approach embodies the following principles:

1. **Strategies used in literacy education can be helpful for teaching children how to code.**
2. **Coding projects can provide opportunities for children's sense making and expression of their own voices.**
3. **Problem-solving can serve as a means towards self-expression.**
4. **Coding activities can engage children in thinking about powerful ideas from computer science, as well as other domains.**
5. **The understanding of coding as an activity that engages children in using artificial languages to think in new ways.**

References

Bers, M. U. (2018). *Coding as a playground: Programming and computational thinking in the early childhood classroom.* New York, NY: Routledge Press.

Carnine, L. & Carnine, D. (2004). The interaction of reading skills and science content knowledge when teaching struggling secondary students. *Reading & Writing Quarterly, 20*(2), 203–218.

Chall, J. (1983). *Stages of reading development.* (2nd ed.). New York, NY: McGraw-Hill.

Duke, N. & Pearson, P. D. (2002). Effective practices for developing reading comprehension. In A. Farstrup & S. Samuels (Eds.), *What research has to say about reading instruction.* (3rd ed.). Newark, DE: International Reading Association, 205–242.

Goldenberg, C. (1992). Instructional conversations: Promoting comprehension through discussion. *The Reading Teacher, 46*(4), 316–326.

Goldenberg, C. (2013). Unlocking the research on English learners: What we know - and don't yet know - about effective instruction. *American Educator, 37*(2), 4–11.

Guzdial, M. & Morrison, B. (2016). Seeking to making computing education as available as mathematics or science education. *Communications of the ACM, 59*(11), 31–33.

Kuenzi, J. J. (2008). Science, Technology, Engineering, and Mathematics (STEM) education: Background, federal policy, and legislative action. *Congressional Research Service Reports,* 35.

National Early Literacy Panel. (2008). *Developing early literacy: Report of the National Early Literacy Panel.* Washington, DC: National Institute for Early Literacy.

Papert, S. (1980). *Mindstorms: Children, computers, and powerful ideas.* New York, NY: Basic Books.

Papert, S. (1987). Information technology and education: Computer criticism vs. technocentric thinking. *Information Technology and Education, 16*(1), 22–30.

Vygotsky, L. (2012). *Thought and language.* Cambridge, MA: MIT Press.

Wing, J. M. (2006). Computational thinking. *CACM Viewpoint,* 33–35. Retrieved from www.cs.cmu.edu/afs/cs/usr/wing/www/publications/Wing06.pdf.

Wing, J. M. (2011). Computational thinking. Presented at *IEEE Symposium on Visual Languages and Human-Centric Computing,* 3.

Learn More about Marina's Work

- *Coding as a Playground: Programming and Computational Thinking in the Early Childhood Classroom,* Routledge (2018).
- *The Official ScratchJr Book: Help your Kids Learn to Code,* No Starch Press (2015).
- *Designing Digital Experiences for Positive Youth Development: From playpen to playground,* Oxford University Press (2012).
- *Blocks to Robots: Learning with Technology in the Early Childhood Classroom,* Teachers College Press (2008).

Marina Recommends

- The ScratchJr app http://scratchjr.org
- The KIBO robot http://scratchjr.org

Chapter 11

Personalized Education and Technology

How Can We Find an Optimal Balance?

Natalia Kucirkova

Introduction

Personalized versus standardized education: which one do you prefer? That's a loaded question for sure, since standardized education has become associated with inflexible accountability measures for teachers and testing overload for children. With the renewed interest in creativity and child-centered learning, standardized education seems to present the perfect foil for the adoption of personalized education: personalized education promises to offer tailored and flexible frameworks for teachers and choice-led curriculum for children.

With the advent of affordable and ubiquitous personal mobile devices, personalized education became the new kid on the educational reform block. Technology has always been part of the interest to transform old educational paradigms. However, the personalized versus standardized education dichotomy is misplaced: to foster holistic outcomes in complex environments, we need combined, not reduced, versions of education. In this essay, I will try to convince you that we need both sides of the educational coin and both strong design and pedagogy.

First, we need to agree that technology-driven education might sound seductive to technology investors and some disillusioned professionals, but it cannot be the driving force in sustainable education models. Technology-driven education emphasizes design rather than pedagogy. Such myopic approaches to technology deployment are characterized by large investments made into hardware rather than professional training and pedagogical support of technology use. My education alarm goes off every time I hear a company claiming to have developed a product which will "transform" children's learning overnight. In my work and in this chapter, I take the approach that technology can mediate and enrich, but not replace or determine, teachers' expertise in the classroom.

Technology-Mediated Education

The role of technology in supporting standardized education is clear: broadly speaking, technology can support organized progression of students across levels, shared benchmarks for student performance and specific guidelines for teaching foundational skills. But what about the role of technology in personalized education?

The key benefits of personalized education center around giving children choices, motivating them to learn and fostering their curiosity, wonder and enjoyment of learning. Technology can support these benefits, but it needs to be designed and applied in a carefully planned way. Let's have a closer look at how this could happen.

> **"The key benefits of personalized education center around giving children choices, motivating them to learn and fostering their curiosity, wonder and enjoyment of learning."**

Personalization and Information Reduction

Technology allows for access to unprecedented amounts of content that could potentially be of significant learning value, but this content needs to be curated and presented in a meaningful sequence. A focus on what is personally important and meaningful for an individual channels attention to a specific piece of information. Personalized education could thus help with the information overload that characterizes the "information age" (Shenk, 1997).

However, if we are to filter information, we need to be clear about the rules that govern the final recommendation. Who decides what information counts as true, popular or "recommended"? You will be familiar with the scandals that have plagued technology giants' monopoly in personalizing information online. The threats around information manipulation for political or commercial ends couldn't be greater than in the age of global nationalism. We can see the effects of extreme personalization on social media where the design supports self-selected groups. Overly personalized environments create powerful in-group biases and expose their members only to confirmatory evidence. In such groups, diversity of views is treated as a justification for an opposite perspective, rather than as a discovery process of alternative possibilities. In education, decades of research show that it is by wrestling with ideas we don't agree with and by taking part in activities we do not necessarily want to take part in, that we refine our own values, rein in our impulses and learn to empathize. From time immemorial schools have therefore been designed as community spaces, not as individual units.

> **"In education, decades of research show that it is by wrestling with ideas we don't agree with and by taking part in activities we do not necessarily want to take part in, that we refine our own values, rein in our impulses and learn to empathize."**

Technology companies that design digital personalized education products such as content recommendation platforms (e.g., Epic!) or entire systems for schools and parents (e.g., Maple) are important because children cannot be expected to fend for themselves in finding the best content online, especially not when it comes to digital reading and "educational" apps that are part of an exploitative commercial model. In addition, recommendation systems need to make sure that they do not reduce diversity to small isolated circles of self-defined interests. For example, in the context of book reading recommendations, if the system restricts the content too much according to specific age groups or reading levels, it might alienate readers, but if it leaves the content unrestricted, it confuses them and does not foster discernment of quality. A significant strategy, and in some cases, an important selling point, is therefore to use recommender algorithms that are embedded in personalized technologies to motivate children to learn.

Personalization and Motivation

Personalization is a useful technique for motivating learners to take part in activities they might not want to or are not interested in (Wigfield & Guthrie, 2000). For example, personalized books motivate reluctant readers to read. When focused on a specific activity, personal motivation can help children succeed in a task or game.

However, the old adage "no pain no gain" rings true when we look at motivation and long-term effects of personalization. Motivation is great for children's initial interest or enjoyment of a learning activity. However, it is through a conscious effort that we can break with our existing schemas and solidify new information in memory. Therefore, learning needs to be both personalized and non-personalized and the two need to be carefully employed in different contexts.

If we used technology for motivational ends only, we might support children's learning interests but not necessarily their learning. There is also the issue of equity and personalized learning. Students who are already motivated to learn might find it helpful to pursue their specialized education with personalized recommendations. However, for children who are falling behind, struggle to identify their interests or perhaps have unhealthy interests, personalization driven by technology and no adult guidance might exacerbate the educational divides (Roberts-Mahoney, Means & Garrison, 2016).

> **"If we used technology for motivational ends only, we might support children's learning interests but not necessarily their learning."**

You might think that the optimal solution would be technology-mediated personalization combined with teachers' guidance. The problem with that solution is that it would require more, not less, teachers' time and professional development (and both are in short supply worldwide). So, what could technology-mediated personalization be used for? To answer this question, we need to look at what strong pedagogies look like. This is where we learn that strategic use of technology-mediated personalization can add to the benefits of standardized education. The combination of personalized education with plural, diverse and equitable education is what colleagues and I call "personalized pluralization".

Personalized Pluralization

The optimal educational system is one where individuality and diversity intersect or where the personal and plural are given equal weight (Bruner, 1996). In personalized pluralization (PP), personalization is applied in small doses within, not at the expense of, standardized curriculum. Such a participatory model of PP is a reciprocal model, in which teachers, designers and researchers all work together in one trio of collaboration. Community-led PP might sound like a lot of academic jargon removed from reality. I am not suggesting that we have all stakeholders collaborate overnight and all the time. But if we keep the combination of participation, personalization and pluralization as our three key overarching goals, then we can engage in fruitful conversation with one another and identify our own role in the collaborations.

For example, as a researcher, I would want to work with designers and teachers (participation) to make sure that technologies are designed using the most cutting-edge tools to motivate children to learn (personalization), but, at the same time expose them to educational challenges and tricky concepts (pluralization). Teachers might want to ensure that they are positioned as valued collaborators in refining the technology design as well as when evaluating the actual technology use in their classrooms.

> **"If we keep the combination of participation, personalization and pluralization as our three key overarching goals, then we can engage in fruitful conversation with one another and identify our own role in the collaborations."**

It is with attention paid to participatory PP that I would like you to contemplate the following example. It draws on my work with children's personalized books, which is an ongoing effort of several researchers, designers and teachers in the UK and the USA. Let me first introduce you to personalized books.

Personalized Books

Personalized books have been tailored, either in their content or form, to an individual reader. Personalized books can contain readers' names, pictures or, when produced digitally, readers' own voice-overs and interactive features. My early research found that paper-based personalized books, which contain the child's own name, favorite items (such as food and places to visit) and pictures, can support children's word learning more than the same books without these personalization features (Kucirkova, Messer & Sheehy, 2014).

We have also found that personalized books can motivate children to read, and often become their favorite books over time. These are important benefits. However, let us not forget that personalized books are part and parcel of children's typical reading diets, which are based on non-personalized books. It is easy to develop preference for a novel item and to pay attention to books that are different from the rest. If we used personalized books without traditional books (that are standardized for all children's enjoyment), we would throw the baby out with the bathwater.

In designing children's digital personalized books, we were mindful of not falling into the trap of technology-driven personalized education. You may have come across the so-called personalized books that are marketed to offer children "magical experiences" by substituting the character's name with the child's name or inserting the child's photo into one of its pages. Personalized books that merely inject the child's name or face for motivational tactics or bespoke gifts are not aligned with the personalized personalization model. However, personalized books that are co-created by family members or teachers, educational professionals, librarians or teaching assistants, can bring about measurable benefits. Such personalized books can be based on fictional or autobiographical stories or on a topic taught in the class. The key is that they are tailored to a particular child's experience or need, they encourage their curiosity and creativity.

The process of making personalized books is like making cakes: there are thousands of recipes and personal tastes. Personalized books can be created using paper-based "ingredients", including cut-out pictures, drawings, collage and art materials. In addition to text and pictures, digital personalized books also contain sounds and interactive features. Moreover, digital personalized books can be archived and shared with others. If you prefer digital personalized books and are looking for some tools to make them, you might find the Our Story app useful.

The key defining characteristic of Our Story is that the app is open-ended, so there are no templates for specific stories; children and adults can make any story they wish to share. The interactions that empowered children and honored their agency were those which followed the so-called 5As of Personalization (Kucirkova, 2017): authorship, autonomy, authenticity, aesthetics and attachment. In these interactions, the children were positioned as the story Authors, they had Autonomy in orchestrating the story-composing process, drawing on their Authentic experiences and their own Aesthetic choices, developing ownership of and Attachment to their final story. These 5As were supported with teachers' mediation, guidance and co-creation of the stories.

"5As of Personalization: authorship, autonomy, authenticity, aesthetics and attachment."

Unlike some story-making apps or learning platforms that position teachers as monitors and curators of children's digital content, the PP model emphasizes teachers' own agency and expertise in communicating their pedagogical knowledge to the child. It positions educational professionals as mentors, listeners and co-producers of children's content (Kucirkova & Cremin, 2017), which is essential for reaping the wider benefits of personalization. With digital personalized books co-created with family members, the educational benefits extend to preserving families' cultural heritage and native language. This is particularly important for multilingual and culturally diverse families who often don't get the opportunity to share their stories in native language and very rarely see their life experiences reflected in mainstream children's storybooks (Kucirkova, 2016).

When observing the co-creation of digital personalized books in monolingual families, my colleagues and I noticed how it supported shared positive technology use at home. This is an important finding given that technologies tend to be used by children in isolation from other family members. Parents who used Our Story to make their own books with the children needed to negotiate their knowledge with that of children, talk about an appropriate story plot, aesthetically pleasing photos and audio recordings and agree on the final artifact (Kucirkova, Messer, Sheehy & Flewitt, 2013).

Teachers who used the Our Story app combined children's interest with their teaching goals. For example, one teacher encouraged children to personalize a classic story with their own photos and sentences, while teaching correct punctuation (Kucirkova, 2014). There are also important benefits in co-creating or sharing children's personalized stories with parents and teachers.

It is important to note that the positive outcomes did not happen because of the app per se but because of the participatory model in which it was used. Any other open-ended software that allows for multimedia content-making might achieve similar results and I have been encouraging teachers to co-produce digital books in their classrooms using the technologies they have access to, including PCs and PowerPoint or small cameras and printers.

The Future

The danger of swinging the educational pendulum to the personalization extreme is that not only do we lose the benefits of personalization but that we also introduce some significant threats. Seven years of empirical research with Our Story demonstrate that, in some contexts, technologies can recraft the delicate balance between personalization and pluralization. We don't know how to negotiate this balance in different contexts, different groups of children and for different learning purposes. What we do know is that we need the best of all four elements – personalization, pluralization, humans and technology – to figure it out.

Natalia's Essentials

1. **Personalized education works best in conjunction with standardized education.**
2. **Personalized books can extend literacy provision to diverse contents contributed by families and communities.**
3. **Personalized books can enrich children's reading, but they need to be used and designed strategically.**
4. **Teachers' active role is indispensable in ensuring the right amalgam of traditional and innovative pedagogical approaches.**

References

Bruner, J. S. (1996). *The culture of education*. Boston: Harvard University Press.

Kucirkova, N. (2014). *iPads and Tablets in the classroom: Personalising children's stories* (Vol. 41). Leicester: UKLA Minibook.

Kucirkova, N. (2016). Personalisation: A theoretical possibility to reinvigorate children's interest in storybook reading and facilitate greater book diversity. *Contemporary Issues in Early Childhood*, 17(3), 304–316.

Kucirkova, N. (2017). How can digital personal(ised) books enrich the language arts curriculum? *The Reading Teacher*, 71(3), 275–284.

Kucirkova, N., & Cremin, T. (2017). Personalised reading for pleasure with digital libraries: Towards a pedagogy of practice and design. *Cambridge Journal of Education*, 48(5), 571–589.

Kucirkova, N., Messer, D., & Sheehy, K. (2014). Reading personalised books with preschool children enhances their word acquisition. *First Language*, 34(3), 227–243.

Kucirkova, N., Messer, D., Sheehy, K., & Flewitt, R. (2013). Sharing personalized stories on iPads: A close look at one parent–child interaction. *Literacy*, 47(3), 115–122.

Roberts-Mahoney, H., Means, A. J., & Garrison, M. J. (2016). Netflixing human capital development: Personalized learning technology and the corporatization of K-12 education. *Journal of Education Policy*, 31(4), 405–420.

Shenk, D. (1997). *Data smog: Surviving the information glut*. New York: HarperCollins Publishers.

Wigfield, A., & Guthrie, J. T. (2000). Engagement and motivation in reading. In M. L. Kamil, P. B. Mosenthal, P. D. Pearson, & R. Bar (eds), *Handbook of reading research* (Vol. 3), pp. 403–422. New York: Routledge.

Learn More about Natalia's Work

Kucirkova, N. (2017). *Digital personalization in early childhood: Impact on childhood*. London: Bloomsbury Publishing. www.bloomsburycollections.com/book/digital-personalization-in-early-childhood-impact-on-childhood/

Kucirkova, N. (2018) *How and why to read and create digital books: A guide for primary practitioners.* London: UCL Press. www.ucl.ac.uk/ucl-press/browse-books/how-and-why-to-read-and-create-childrens-digital-books/

Natalia Recommends

- Cremin, T., Mottram, M., Collins, F. M., Powell, S., & Safford, K. (2014). *Building communities of engaged readers: Reading for pleasure.* New York: Routledge.
- Ninio, A., & Snow, C. E. (1996). *Pragmatic development.* Boulder: Westview Press. (*Pragmatic Development* is an edited book and the list of contributors include my favorite learning scientists who build on the rich work of Lev Vygotsky and study the importance of dialogue and conversation in the classroom, including: Professors Roger Saljo, Michael Cole, James Wertsch, Luis C. Moll, Neil Mercer, Karen Littleton and many others.)
- Faulkner, D., Woodhead, M., & Littleton, K. (2013). *Learning relationships in the classroom.* New York: Routledge.

Chapter 12

Makerspaces in the Early Years
Enhancing Digital Literacy and Creativity

Jackie Marsh

Having undertaken research on the digital literacy practices of young children over the last two decades, it is, perhaps, inevitable that I currently find myself leading a series of research projects related to 'makerspaces'. These are spaces that enable participants to create a range of artefacts using specialist tools and resources, such as electronics, laser cutters and 3D printers, alongside everyday resources. There has been interest in recent years in the role of digital 'making', the design and production of digital artefacts, texts and products (Blikstein, 2013; Dougherty, 2013; Johnson, Adams Becker, Estrada and Freeman, 2015; Peppler, Halverson and Kafai, 2016), alongside a rise in the provision of fabrication labs (Fab Labs), or 'makerspaces', open-access spaces in which people use equipment such as 3D printers and laser cutters for these purposes. A New Media Consortium Horizon report suggests that such spaces have 'the potential to empower young people to become agents of change in their communities' (Johnson et al., 2015). Makerspaces are part of the move to a do-it-yourself (DIY) culture in which citizens take the initiative and become more self-sufficient, made possible through the development of new digital tools and practices. Rather than this being experienced as an individual process, however, makerspaces emphasize collaboration and sharing.

The inevitability of this as a current research focus arises from the fact that having spent many hours observing digital making of all kinds, as children seek to make meaning through the creation of digital texts and artefacts, it became clear to me that making is important not simply for the acquisition of skills and knowledge, but also for the development of a 'maker mind-set'. This enables children to explore, take risks, reflect and problem-solve, important skills and attributes for the age of the fourth industrial revolution (Brown-Martin, 2017). If we view digital literacy as a social practice in which children engage in meaning-making practices in order to express themselves and communicate with others, then it seems appropriate to extend the modes and media available for this to include new technologies, such as digital fabrication tools. In addition, it is important to consider the use of symbolic systems other than written language, such as is the case when coding, in the creative process. In one sense, makerspaces are nothing new in early childhood education; early years settings have always fostered children's playful meaning-making using a range of art and craft materials, wood, bricks and so on. However, the extension of the concept into the contemporary digital landscape offers new possibilities for children's creativity.

> **"If we view digital literacy as a social practice in which children engage in meaning-making practices in order to express themselves and communicate with others, then it seems appropriate to extend the modes and media available for this to include new technologies, such as digital fabrication tools."**

The 'MakEY' (Makerspaces in the Early Years: Enhancing Digital Literacy and Creativity) project has involved seven European countries, working with partners from across the world. The countries involved are running makerspaces for young children in kindergartens, schools, libraries, museums and community centers. The contexts and settings are varied and, thus, a wide range of approaches are being adopted across the various countries. The project I am directly involved in, in Sheffield, a northern city in England, aimed to examine the potential value that makerspaces have for early years settings.

In order to offer an insight into the value of makerspaces for young children, I will draw on a case study conducted with one primary class of six- and seven-year olds. The focus of the project was on the Moomins, central characters in a series of books written by the Finnish author Tove Jansson. A travelling puppet theatre company first came to the school, to share some magical Moomin stories with the children. Pupils then drew characters for their own Moomin puppet shows, which were laser cut out of wood and inserted into shoeboxes. The children learned about electrical circuits as they created backlights for their Moomin theatres. They wrote play scripts for their productions, and a few performed their plays for the school in an assembly. Finally, the children moulded Moomin characters out of clay and used a scanner app to make 3D digital models of their characters. These were printed off as models using a 3D printer. The 3D-printed models became the central characters in digital, green screen animations. The children then imported images of their 3D models into a virtual reality app, Google Tilt Brush, where they created virtual Moomin valleys around their 3D Moomins.

These activities involved the children in making use of some of the tools and practices found in Fab Labs, but they also included digital making activities that children were familiar with (e.g. animated films) in addition to traditional literacy practices. This, I would argue, is a valuable model of a makerspace – one in which children move fluidly across a range of modes and media in their meaning-making. This project was very much focused on the outcomes, as that is what the school wanted, but makerspaces need not necessarily do so – children also had opportunities to play in open-ended ways with materials in many of the makerspaces run as part of the project.

"This, I would argue, is a valuable model of a makerspace – one in which children move fluidly across a range of modes and media in their meaning-making."

Makerspaces are important in terms of children acquiring subject knowledge across a wide range of areas utilizing this STEAM (STEM subjects alongside arts and design) approach. In relation to young children and technology, makerspaces can offer young children opportunities to engage in some of the technological practices that will become more significant in the future, such as digital fabrication (3D printing, laser cutting, vinyl cutting), robotics (coding) and Virtual Reality (VR). The makerspace approach means that the technologies are not used simply for their own sake but are embedded into meaningful practices that enable children to make connections across areas of learning.

Makerspaces pose challenges for some elements of schooling. Ideally, children need time to tinker, hack and play, and be able to return to projects in an iterative manner, but sometimes the structures of the schoolday mitigate against this. In addition, space is often at a premium in schools and kindergartens, and so it is difficult to leave equipment out for open access, not to mention the prohibitive cost of some of the equipment required. In some of the settings involved in the MakEY projects, pop-up makerspaces were utilized, facilitated by the use of a simple trolley, packed full with materials, that was wheeled into the classroom. One of the features of the MakEY project that was of value was the linking up of early years settings with staff who work in makerspaces. This enabled schools and kindergartens access to materials and skills that they did not possess. Of course, not all towns and cities have Fab Labs and makerspaces, and so this is only an option for a limited number of settings.

Implications for Research, Policy and Practice

In terms of future developments, there are a number of implications of this work for research, policy and practice. First, in terms of research, there is a need to explore further the kinds of learning which occur in makerspaces. In the MakEY project, we have been mapping young children's learning using observation and documentation (field notes, photographs and video). Some of the children have also worn GoPro chestcams, which have enabled the capture of their interactions with a range of media and technologies, and so can inform assessment practices. But there is more work to do in this area, particularly in relation to the assessment of learning in out-of-school makerspaces, and how this information is then made available to interested staff in kindergartens and schools. Second, there are implications for policy and practice. Early childhood teacher education needs to consider the role and value of makerspaces in early learning and provide opportunities for pre-service teachers to develop knowledge and skills in this area. In-service teachers would also benefit from related professional development, and from investment by early years settings into the kinds of equipment of value in makerspaces. Finally, the MakEY project has demonstrated that young children can engage meaningfully with technologies that have not been developed with them in mind, such as 3D printers and laser cutters. However, there is further work to do in developing interfaces that enable children to move their ideas into production much more easily. This approach will need collaboration between early childhood academics and industry partners in order to develop tools and apps that are fit for purpose. Not to do so is to risk our youngest citizens being excluded from some of the exciting possibilities that new technologies offer. As we move ever more steadily into the future of post-digital literacies (Apperley, Jayemanne and Nansen, 2016), in which the ability to move seamlessly across digital, non-digital and online/offline domains as we produce and consume texts and artefacts is key, then the value of offering young children opportunities to hack, make and tinker in makerspaces becomes clear.

Acknowledgment

MakEY is funded by the EU H2020 Programme, Project Number 734720.

Jackie's Essentials

1. **Provide opportunities for children to tinker, hack and make in makerspaces.** Provide spaces that enable them to explore using a wide range of technologies and materials. Such spaces need not be 'high-tech', it is more about fostering experimentation and risk-taking while engaged in hands-on making.
2. **Recognize that play is an important part of any makerspace for young children.** Allow space and opportunities for play to emerge, both individual play with the materials and collaborative play as children interact with each other.
3. **Engage children in reflection on their learning in makerspaces.** Record their practices with cameras and use the photographs to prompt discussion with children on what they were doing and what they thought about what they were doing.
4. **Consider running after-school makerspaces to which parents and family members are invited.** Intergenerational making is good for strengthening relationships and enabling family members to have fun together.
5. **Be attentive to issues of social inclusion.** Ensure the tools, materials and topics draw from children's own social and cultural practices. Scaffold the experiences in appropriate ways for children with specific needs.

References

Apperley, T., Jayemanne, D., and Nansen, B. (2016). Postdigital literacies: Materiality, mobility and the aesthetics of recruitment. In B. Parry, C. Burnett, and G. Merchant (Eds.), *Literacy, media, technology: Past, present and future*. London: Bloomsbury Publishing, pp. 203–218.

Blikstein, P. (2013). Digital fabrication and 'making' in education: The democratization of invention. In J. Walter-Herrmann and C. Büching (Eds.), *FabLab: Of machines, makers and inventors*. Bielefeld: Transcript Publishers, pp. 203–222.

Brown-Martin, G. (2017). *Education and the fourth industrial revolution: White paper for the TFO*. Toronto, Ontario: Groupe Média TFO. Retrieved from: www.groupeme diatfo.org/wp-content/uploads/2017/12/FINAL-Education-and-the-Fourth-Indus trial-Revolution-1-1-1.pdf.

Dougherty, D. (2013). The maker mindset. In M. Honey and D. E. Kanter (Eds.), *Design, make, play: Growing the next generation of STEM innovators*. New York, NY and Abingdon, Oxon: Routledge, (pp. 7–11).

Johnson, L., Adams Becker, S., Estrada, V., and Freeman, A. (2015). *NMC Horizon report: 2015 K-12 edition*. Austin, TX: The New Media Consortium. Retrieved from: http://cdn.nmc.org/media/2015-nmc-horizon-report-k12-EN.pdf.

Peppler, K., Halverson, E., and Kafai, Y. (Eds.) (2016). *Makeology: Makerspaces as learning environments* (Volume 1& 2). New York, NY: Routledge.

Learn More about Jackie's Work

- MakEY website http://makeyproject.eu
- Marsh, J., Kumpulainen, K., Nisha, B., Velicu, A., Blum-Ross, A., Hyatt, D., Jónsdóttir, S. R., Levy, R., Little, S., Marusteru, G., Ólafsdóttir, M. E., Sandvik, K., Scott, F., Thestrup, K., Arnseth, H. C., Dýrfjörð, K., Jornet, A., Kjartansdóttir, S. H., Pahl, K., Pétursdóttir, S., and Thorsteinsson, G. (2017). *Makerspaces in the early years: A literature review*. University of Sheffield: MakEY Project. Retrieved from: http://makeyproject.eu/wp-content/uploads/2017/02/ Makey_Literature_Review.pdf
- Lahmar, J., Taylor, M., Marsh, J., Jakobsdóttir, S., Velicu, A., Arnseth, H. C., Blum-Ross, A., Dýrfjörð, K., Gissurardóttir, S., Hjartarson, T., Jónsdóttir, S. R., Kjartansdóttir, S. H., Kumpulainen, K., Mitarcă, M., Ólafsdóttir, M. E., Pétursdóttir, S., Sandvik, K., Thestrup, K., and Thorsteinsson, G. (2017). *Makerspaces in the early years: Current perceptions and practices of early years practitioners, library and museum educators and makerspace staff*. University of Sheffield: MakEY Project. Retrieved from: http://makeyproject.eu/wp-content/uploads/2018/01/ MakEY_Survey.pdf

Jackie Recommends

- Brahms, L., and Werner, J. (2013). Designing makerspaces for family learning in museums and science centers. In M. Honey and D. E. Kanter (Eds.), *Design, make, play: Growing the next generation of stem innovators*. New York, NY and Abingdon, Oxon: Routledge.

- Gauntlett, D. (2011). *Making is connecting: The social meaning of creativity, from DIY and knitting to YouTube and Web 2.0*. Cambridge: Polity Press.
- Kress, G. (2010). *Multimodality*. London: Routledge.
- Peppler, K., Halverson, E., and Kafai, Y. (Eds.). (2016). *Makeology: Makerspaces as learning environments* (Volumes 1 & 2). New York, NY: Routledge.
- Wohlwend, K. E., Peppler, K. A., and Keune, A. (2016). Design playshop: Pre-schoolers making, playing and learning with squishy circuits. In K. A. Peppler, Y. B. Kafai, and E. R. Halverson (Eds.), *Makeology: Makers as learners*. New York, NY: Routledge.

Chapter 13

Mobile Media and Parent–Child Interaction

Jenny Radesky

Introduction

In pediatric training, clinicians start to recognize the hot-button topics that can make parents feel uncertain and judged. These include discipline, their child's difficult behavior, feeding problems, sleeping problems, and digital media. Each of these issues is enmeshed in family dynamics, parents' own childhood experiences, socioeconomic status, and how well parents can self-regulate in moments of child distress. So, if we approach one of these topics with a one-size-fits-all lecture, as if there is one 'right' answer, parents will often disengage. Meeting parents *where they are* is essential for effective communication about difficult topics.

But why is media such a hot-button topic for parents? In addition to the general anxiety parents feel about their child's success and well-being, there is the added stress of living in the midst of incredibly rapid evolution of digital technologies. Rich Ling (2004), writing about the global uptake of mobile communication, argued that novel technologies always induce societal anxiety by disrupting our usual routines, communication approaches, and information exchange, until we adapt technology design affordances to suit our values. Since that time, technological innovation has quickened exponentially (e.g., Pokemon Go reached 50 million global users within 16 days), faster than we can study it. As a result, this disruption of norms has contributed to public discourses that often include emotional arguments or judgment of parents.

> **"Meeting parents where they are is essential for effective communication about difficult topics."**

When discussing difficult topics in clinic, parents are much more engaged when we talk about *their specific experience* and *their specific child* – rather than vagaries of 'parenting style' or being a 'low-tech parent.' Parents want to know what to say, how to react, what to do *in the moment*. The infant mental health framework – in which I was trained – is far more relevant to parents' lived experiences because it takes into account what the individual child and parent bring to the table, and how this shapes their interactions. When it comes to media, it is easier for parents to engage in discussions about how and when media intersects with their daily routines and interacts with their child, for better or for worse, rather than think about media as a 'risk factor' they need to avoid. For this reason, this framework has become the underpinning of my research questions.

Mobile Devices and Dyadic Interactions

Our first effort to examine mobile media use through a dyadic lens was an exploratory, nonparticipant observational study in fast-food restaurants (Radesky et al., 2014). We chose an anthropologic methodology because we wanted to first describe this novel phenomenon – not test it with preconceived, potentially biased, hypotheses. After three months of writing field notes about 55 families with young children in Boston-area restaurants, we observed the same patterns again and again: parents, when highly absorbed in their mobile devices (especially when scrolling or texting), showed little positive engagement with their children. We repeatedly observed that, during parent device absorption, conversation was minimal, or children would attempt to get parents' behavior and get no, delayed, or overreacting responses.

> **"Parents, when highly absorbed in their mobile devices (especially when scrolling or texting), showed little positive engagement with their children."**

Why were these parents getting absorbed with their devices, we wondered? Was it something in the device that they couldn't take their eyes off of? Was it a workday and they needed to attend to email? Were they withdrawing from irritating child behavior or was this just a marker of parenting style? To find out, we next tested associations between parent mobile device use and parent–child interactions during a videotaped feeding task – a 20-minute, moderately boring feeding task during which 23% of parents spontaneously brought out their mobile device. Device-using parents were no different from non-device-users in terms of depression symptoms, parenting style, or any other sociodemographic variable – however, they showed significantly fewer verbal and nonverbal interactions with their children and less encouraging interactions (Radesky et al., 2015). In a later study, even after accounting for factors like co-parenting quality and parenting stress, we found that parent technology interference during parent–child activities predicted more child internalizing and externalizing behaviors, both in the moment and over time (McDaniel & Radesky, 2018a, 2018b).

With an infant mental health framework in mind, we then wondered what was driving parents to bring mobile devices into interpersonal spaces, which could potentially disrupt parent–child connection during family meals, playtime, car rides, and other routines important to child social-emotional development. One explanation is that technology interference is a reflection of underlying parent–child relationship difficulties. For example, mobile device-using parents in the above feeding task study expressed less understanding of their child's motivations or personality; they expressed more of a sense that their child was 'difficult' compared to parents who didn't use a mobile device during the task (Radesky et al., 2018). Perhaps these parents were less aware of their child's experience of technology interference or were intentionally withdrawing from the child for stress relief; or perhaps repeated disrupted parent–child interactions made it harder to read their child's cues or had triggered more attention-seeking behavior. Our recent longitudinal study (McDaniel & Radesky, 2018b) suggests that both occur; difficult child behavior predicts more parent technology interference, which in turn predicts later child behavior problems. In interviews, parents also report feeling information overload, stress with toggling between child bids and the demands contained in their mobile device and feeling that their devices are at once both stress-relieving and stress-inducing (Radesky et al., 2016). Persuasive design may be central to this parent experience and the phenomenon of technology interference.

Parent–Child–Device Triad? Computers as Social Actors and Persuasive Design

The ideas of computers as social actors (Nass, Steuer & Tauber, 1994) and persuasive design (Fogg, 2002) both originated at Stanford University in the 1990s, when it became clear that embedding social features in computer communication can motivate user behavior. At the time, it was hoped that persuasive design – interacting with user psychology via rewards (social feedback, tokens) and behavioral nudges – could help users engage in healthier or prosocial behaviors. Since then, persuasive design has also come to mean the attention-grabbing 'clickbait' and engaging features intended to prolong user engagement (e.g., omitting the clock from screen interfaces) that don't necessarily serve the user's best interests, but are effective marketing tools. Users are not always aware of their motivations for these habit-driven, subconscious processes – which can make it difficult for parents to self-regulate their own technology use or teach their child to do the same.

In interviews, we found that parents talk about how such design features split their attention, make them feel drawn back to their device in ways that interrupt daily routines, or feeling 'hooked' (Radesky et al., 2016). With their work, social lives, stress relief, and news of the world all contained in one handheld computer, parents describe finding it hard to create boundaries or anticipate when they would get 'sucked in' or stressed out by 'the whole world in their lap.' In fact, parents appreciated the opportunity to take part in our focus groups, to step back and reflect upon their family's technology-use habits, which had become more reactive and less intentional, over time.

But, without conscious reflection about parents' own relationships with their mobile devices, it will be difficult to ask parents to become the media mentors for their children that we hope they will be.

Moreover, emerging research suggests that persuasive design affects parents' ability to scaffold or co-view with their young children during digital play. Although our pediatric recommendations encourage parents to co-view and co-play with children, persuasive design appeared to make this more difficult in our videotaped observational study (Hiniker et al., 2018). Compared to traditional toys or open-ended creative apps (e.g., Toca Kitchen), parents struggled to get responses from preschoolers playing fast-paced gamified apps or share space with children around the tablet – often craning their necks to see the tablet nestled in their children's laps or giving up attempts to engage.

> **"Without conscious reflection about parents' own relationships with their mobile devices, it will be difficult to ask parents to become the media mentors for their children that we hope they will be."**

Conclusions: The Importance of Parent Digital Literacy

This moment of parent digital overwhelm also represents an opportunity to engage parents constructively, for them to learn digital literacy themselves and pass this knowledge along to their children through direct teaching and role modeling. It is important to have conversations with parents that help them to build self-awareness of their relationship with their mobile devices; critically evaluate the media they and their children consume; recognize and resist the 'hook' of persuasive design when it undermines rather than empowers them; and to use media together with children. In addition, parents can be empowered to place consumer pressure on poorly designed technology that is hindering, rather than supporting, their values or whose affordances seem designed to meet commercial goals rather than family goals. Rather, we can encourage parents to carve out time to single-task on family activities, and also to choose products whose design respects their child's mind and their own role in media mentoring.

Jenny's Essentials

When talking with parents about media use:

1. **Recognize the polarization around discussions of media use and child development.** Normalize the experience of feeling overwhelmed by the flood of new technologies and try to frame the discussion about the parent's specific experience.

2. **Help parents think about the motivations behind media that occur on a daily basis** and how this might reflect parenting stress or difficult child behavior, and what alternate approaches they could use for managing those times of distress.

3. **Help parents think about their digital play experiences with children** – which ones create a space for them and allow them to easily transfer learning to the rest of the child's world, which ones elbow them out or make it hard to interact during play – and make content choices this way.

4. **Help parents build digital literacy** around the persuasive and tricky features of interactive media that grab their attention, try to prolong their usage, keep them coming back regularly, or make them lose awareness of time – so they can teach their children the same.

5. **Help parents build unplugged times for all family members** – this may include 'do not disturb' device settings or WiFi turnoffs, or just putting mobile devices in a basket. This will allow parents to be media mentors in terms of their informal teaching and role modeling of device use.

References

Fogg, B. J. (2002). Persuasive technology: Using computers to change what we think and do. *Ubiquity, 2002*(December), 5.

Hiniker, A., Lee, B., Kientz, J. A., & Radesky, J. S. (2018, April). Let's play!: Digital and analog play between preschoolers and parents. In *Proceedings of the 2018 CHI Conference on Human Factors in Computing Systems* (p. 659). ACM.

Ling, R. (2004). *The mobile connection: The cell phone's impact on society.* Amsterdam, Netherlands: Elsevier.

McDaniel, B. T., & Radesky, J. S. (2018a). Technoference: Parent distraction with technology and associations with child behavior problems. *Child Development, 89*(1), 100–109.

McDaniel, B. T., & Radesky, J. S. (2018b). Technoference: Longitudinal associations between parent technology use, parenting stress, and child behavior problems. *Pediatric Research, 84*(2),210-218.

Nass, C., Steuer, J., & Tauber, E. R. (1994, April). Computers are social actors. In *Proceedings of the SIGCHI Conference on Human Factors in Computing Systems* (pp. 72–78). ACM.

Radesky, J., Leung, C., Appugliese, D., Miller, A. L., Lumeng, J. C., & Rosenblum, K. L. (2018). Maternal mental representations of the child and mobile phone use during parent–child mealtimes. *Journal of Developmental & Behavioral Pediatrics, 39*(4), 310–317.

Radesky, J. S., Kistin, C., Eisenberg, S., Gross, J., Block, G., Zuckerman, B., & Silverstein, M. (2016). Parent perspectives on their mobile technology use: The excitement and exhaustion of parenting while connected. *Journal of Developmental & Behavioral Pediatrics, 37*(9), 694–701.

Radesky, J., Miller, A. L., Rosenblum, K. L., Appugliese, D., Kaciroti, N., & Lumeng, J. C. (2015). Maternal mobile device use during a structured parent–child interaction task. *Academic Pediatrics, 15*(2), 238–244.

Radesky, J. S., Kistin, C. J., Zuckerman, B., Nitzberg, K., Gross, J., Kaplan-Sanoff, M., Augustyn, M., & Silverstein, M. (2014). Patterns of mobile device use by caregivers and children during meals in fast food restaurants. *Pediatrics, 133*(4), e843–e849.

Learn More about Jenny's Work

- My recent blog post on persuasive design and kids: https://labblog. uofmhealth.org/health-tech/persuasive-digital-design-appealing-to-adults-problematic-for-kids
- Our article about how to talk to parents and kids about technology when it's there in the room with you: www.jpeds.com/article/S0022-3476(18)30475-X/fulltext
- My blog post about the American Academy of Pediatrics 2016 guidelines: https://theconversation.com/how-should-we-teach-our-kids-to-use-digital-media-67446
- Our commentary about the theoretical concerns and opportunities with mobile and interactive media: http://pediatrics.aappublications. org/content/pediatrics/135/1/1.full.pdf
- Our first study of parent mobile device use during fast-food meals: http://pediatrics.aappublications.org/content/pediatrics/early/2014/03/ 05/peds.2013-3703.full.pdf

Jenny Recommends

- **Barry Zuckerman** on helping parents build self-understanding: Zuckerman B., Zuckerman P. M., Siegel D. J. Promoting self-understanding in parents – for the great good of your patients: help parents discern how much their upbringing affects the parenting they do, and you'll promote a positive parent–child relationship – no small accomplishment! Includes an online Guide for Parents. *Contemporary Pediatrics* 2005 *22*(4): 77–84.
- **Tristan Harris** on persuasive design: www.ted.com/talks/tristan_har ris_the_manipulative_tricks_tech_companies_use_to_capture_your_at tention
- **Scott Campbell** on self-reflection: https://theconversation.com/find ing-solitude-in-an-era-of-perpetual-contact-58750
- **Carrie James** co-creator of the Digital Civics Toolkit: www.teaching channel.org/blog/2018/05/31/the-digital-civics-toolkit/

Chapter 14

No Surprise
Families Matter in Digital-Based Learning

M. Elena Lopez

It is a new day for families. As one who was initially apprehensive about digital tools, I have come to embrace them to connect with my two-year-old grandson who lives in Manila. I use my cell phone to video chat with him as he shows me how he can maneuver his toy cars around the floor or points to his picture books. I find myself creating videos and photo albums of my travels and visits to museums to share with him. New technologies have changed the face of how families connect globally and bring together cultures and time zones in a way never before experienced in history. Not only does technology bring families together, but it is also an important tool for building children's learning and development.

> **"New technologies have changed the face of how families connect globally and bring together cultures and time zones in a way never before experienced in history."**

I've spent many years documenting the ways families create pathways for children's success. For at least 50 years, a large body of research has shown that families matter for children's school readiness and school performance. Parents who hold high educational expectations, engage in activities linked to learning, and partner with teachers, contribute to students' positive academic outcomes. While this pattern endures, the manner in which families demonstrate their educational engagement has evolved and will continue to do so. In part, this is because the ecology of children's learning is changing. Children learn from watching videos, exploring apps, and using tablets. And families use and shape digital tools and media to boost children's learning.

> **"Parents who hold high educational expectations, engage in activities linked to learning, and partner with teachers, contribute to students' positive academic outcomes."**

What Do We Know about Effective Family Engagement Practices? And How Can These Practices Be Enriched through Digital Tools?

Over the past decade, I've seen family engagement altered and expanded by digital technology and tools. First and foremost, I've seen these tools help families feel more confident. Families become engaged in children's learning when they feel confident that they can make a difference. There are nuanced ways in which digital tools boost this confidence. At the Watertown Public Library in Massachusetts, I have observed parents, grandparents, caregivers, and young children jostle for a space on the crowded floor for Nursery Rhyme Time. The librarian draws their attention by singing and inviting everyone to join. As she continues for the next 30 minutes to entertain a rapt audience with stories, songs, and finger puppets, families practice dialogic reading and whip out their cell phones to video the learning experience. The librarian later tells my research team that the videos are shared with other family members and the session is replicated at home and even in the library's outdoor spaces. Learning happens, in part, by watching and observing the behavior of others. Through modeling and practice, as well as continuing behavior imitation, parents are likely to gain more confidence reading with their children.

> **"Families discover how to make the early literacy experience fun and developmentally appropriate; children learn together with their families among a community of caring people; and through digital media, families help librarians extend their influence beyond the library walls."**

What happens in Watertown is a wonderful example of the new ecology of learning. In it, the real and the virtual connect across different contexts and relationships. Families discover how to make the early literacy experience fun and developmentally appropriate; children learn together with their families among a community of caring people; and through digital media, families help librarians extend their influence beyond the library walls.

Second, I've seen digital tools help parent–child interactions that before might have been laden with anxiety and doubt, transformed into fun, dynamic learning interactions. For example, families play a large role in children's early mathematical thinking. But for some parents, reading and talking about math creates anxiety. Innovative digital tools turn math into playful parent–child interactions through stories, activities, and games. Researchers from the Education Development Center (EDC) and SRI International are working with developers at WGBH, a public television station in Boston, to create tablet-based and hands-on activities for preschoolers, teachers, and parents that focus on cultivating children's spatial vocabulary and navigational skills. Project findings show that families enjoy digital and blended activities and children demonstrate more spatial knowledge after using them with their parents (Sherwood & Presser, 2017).

Third, digital media have the potential to make family engagement manageable. Suddenly teachers and families can connect and text with each other and stay in touch with a click of a button. Moreover, given their busy lives and the overwhelming amount of parenting information, families can miss out on important practices. Text messages serve as timely nudges. In the earliest years, platforms like the Text4baby app reminded new parents that they are doing great and provided important time stamps for when to get vaccinations and what to expect at general ages and milestones.

As children transition to kindergarten, digital platforms provide short and specific steps that parents can follow to boost children's kindergarten readiness. Education researchers developed the Ready4K text messaging program and tested it in San Francisco preschools. Results showed an increase in home literacy activities and children's early literacy skills. Texting was particularly beneficial for black and Hispanic parents and children. Inspired by these outcomes, another team of researchers in Pittsburgh developed Connect-Text to address chronic absenteeism in kindergarten and were successful in lowering absenteeism rates (Weiss, Lopez & Caspe, 2018).

Fourth, family engagement is about building community. Very often, educational activities are segregated rather than designed to bring together entire families and generations as well as different socioeconomic groups. Technology holds the promise to bring communities and families together and to create broader social networks. My daughter's Sparklelab (Philippines) welcomes parents, grandparents, and volunteers to serve as mentors, join design workshops, provide food (a must!), and support school-aged children as they learn to code or make LED accessories. Some of these children have special needs; others come from affluent or poor backgrounds and diverse nationalities. Projects are collaborative and children and youth—some with a 13-year age gap—learn the values of sharing, respect, diversity, and teamwork (Lopez, 2015).

Family engagement is foremost a shared responsibility of parents and educators for children's learning. This idea is especially relevant today as new technologies bring promise as well as risks. Many parents of young children believe that media and technology can result in gains in reading and math skills but can also have a negative impact on attention spans and social skills (Center on Media and Human Development, 2014). Parents are turning to family and friends, teachers, and recommendations from schools for guidance in navigating media. Educators, media developers, and community institutions have a responsibility to help parents access quality resources, use them wisely, and set plans for media use.

"Family engagement is foremost a shared responsibility of parents and educators for children's learning."

Public libraries do not immediately come to mind as resources for digital media and learning. Yet, librarians are experts in digital literacies and libraries are home to high-speed internet access. Claudia Haines, the youth services librarian at the Homer Public Library in Alaska, is quoted in Weiss, Caspe, Lopez, and McWilliams (2016).

> "Let's say a family comes into the library with their little person who is a huge dinosaur fan and immediately heads to the dinosaur section to check out books," Haines describes. "My job is to help them access information and media in any format that would support their aspiring paleontologist. So, I might ask, 'Oh, have you seen this audiobook? Do you know about this cool dinosaur app? Did you know that there is a dinosaur expert at the museum next week?'"

Broadly defined, family engagement is also a shared responsibility for all children to have access to rich learning opportunities. Digital tools become tools for public education and advocacy. Through social media platforms, parents voice what matters most for children and families. They bring parent voices not only to point out urgent problems but also the solutions that ensure family well-being. Mom's Rising, for example, advocates for affordable, quality early care and education for all families who need it and a living wage and benefits for the early-childhood workforce.

With a long history of engagement, it is no surprise that families are using digital media to learn together with their children and to boost children's academic and social skills. Families produce video content to expand the learning experiences of children in time and space. They link tablet-based apps with household routines such as preparing lunch and mapping directions to a park. They respond to nudges to guide their children's learning and monitor attendance. They seek ways to improve the access and quality of early-childhood education. These examples by no means cover the full range of ways in which families are exploring digital media. But it should suffice to make the case that digital tools energize families to be proactive in children's learning. The challenge for us educators is to support that engagement.

Elena's Essentials

1. **Keep abreast of research-based family engagement practices**. Use them to innovate and improve children's learning and development with digital tools.
2. **Listen and learn from families.** Use the methods of human-centered design thinking to develop empathy and work together to create rich learning opportunities for all children.

3. **Build a continuing pathway of family engagement** through the school years based on the experience and expertise of the early-childhood field.
4. **Create opportunities**—through programs, apps, and other means—for entire families to learn together by exploring, connecting, and creating via digital tools.
5. **Broaden our perspectives** by learning from global programs.

References

Center on Media and Human Development, School of Communication, Northwestern University. (2014). *Parenting in the age of digital technology: A national survey.* Chicago, IL: Author. Retrieved from https://cmhd.northwestern.edu/wp-content/uploads/2015/06/ParentingAgeDigitalTechnology.REVISED.FINAL_.2014.pdf.

Lopez, R. (2015). Play. Create. Share. Be. Making, learning and youth development. Retrieved from https://static1.squarespace.com/static/5889b407414fb5d0cd583831/t/5890462b20099e5e9e7efe3c/1485850158503/FabLearnSPARKLELAB.pdf.

Sherwood, H., & Presser, A. L. (2017, November 9). Finding their way: Family engagement with digital math activities helps children develops spatial skills [Blog post]. Retrieved from https://globalfrp.org/Articles/Finding-Their-Way-Family-Engagement-with-Digital-Math-Activities-Helps-Children-Develop-Spatial-Skills.

Weiss, H., Lopez, M. E., & Caspe, M. (2018). *Joining together to create a bold vision for next generation family engagement: Engaging families to transform education.* Report for the Carnegie Corporation of New York. Boston, MA: Global Family Research Project.

Weiss, H., Caspe, M., Lopez, M. E., & McWilliams, L. (2016). *Ideabook: Libraries for families.* Cambridge, MA: Harvard Family Research Project. Retrieved from https://globalfrp.org/Articles/Libraries-for-the-21st-Century-It-s-A-Family-Thing.

Learn More about Elena's Work

Caspe, M., & Lopez, M. E. (2018). The 5Rs: Research-based strategies for engaging families in STEM. In M. Caspe, T. A. Woods, & J. Kennedy (Eds.), *Promising practices for engaging families in STEM learning* (pp. 3–17). Charlotte, NC: Information Age Publishing.

Lopez, M. E., Caspe, M. C., & Simpson, C. (2017). Engaging families in public libraries. *Public Library Quarterly, 36*(4), 318–333. doi:10.1080/01616846.2017.1354364.

Lopez, M. E., Caspe, M., & Weiss, H. B. (2017). Logging in to family engagement in the digital age. In C. Donohue (Ed.), *Family engagement in the digital age: Early childhood educators as media mentors* (pp. 58–73). New York, NY: Routledge.

Weiss, H., Lopez, M. E., & Caspe, M. (2018). *Joining together to create a bold vision for next generation family engagement: Engaging families to transform education.* Report for the Carnegie Corporation of New York. Boston, MA: Global Family Research Project. Retrieved from https://globalfrp.org/Articles/Joining-Together-to-Create-a-Bold-Vision-for-Next-Generation-Family-Engagement-Engaging-Families-to-Transform-Education

Weiss, H. B., & Lopez, M. E. (2015). Engage families for anywhere, anytime learning. *Phi Delta Kappan, 96*(7), 14–19.

Weiss, H. B., Lopez, M. E., Kreider, H., & Chatman-Nelson, C. (2014). *Preparing educators to engage families: Case studies using an ecological systems framework.* Thousand Oaks, CA: Sage.

Elena Recommends

Brown, T. (2009). *Change by design.* New York, NY: HarperCollins.

Bryk, A. S., Gomez, L. M., Grunow, A., & LeMahieu, P. G. (2015). *Learning to improve: How America's school can get better at getting better.* Cambridge, MA: Harvard Education Press.

Small, M. L. (2009). *Unanticipated gains: Origins of network inequality in everyday life.* New York, NY: Oxford University Press.

Chapter 15

A Mission for Media Mentors
Creating Critical Thinkers

Lisa Guernsey

One day, not too long ago, in a small kindergarten classroom in Washington, DC, a group of children decided to plant tomatoes. To get started, they turned to one of the parents who was assisting in the class that day. Little did they know that the mother they asked, Vivian Maria Vasquez, was an international expert on inquiry-based learning. She did not tell them how to plant tomatoes. Instead, she took the group—which included her son, T.J.—on an odyssey that started with searches through books and on the internet. Their searching led them to discover that tomato plants could be grown all kinds of ways. They could plant seeds directly into the ground, they could transplant small seedlings from containers into the ground, and they could even buy a device advertised on television called the Topsy Turvy Tomato Planter®, which involved growing tomato plants upside down.

T.J. and his classmates found that last fact to be most fascinating. Can plants really grow upside down? They found a YouTube video of the television commercial and listened closely to its claims. The video showed a man digging in the ground to plant tomatoes the traditional way and holding his back in pain. The voice-over talked about "back-breaking work." The next image showed a smiling woman using the Topsy Turvy Tomato Planter® while not even breaking a sweat.

The children had even more questions now. What is back-breaking work? Why is a man the one doing the shoveling? Would it be better to use this Topsy Turvy device than to plant seeds in the ground? Would it work? Vasquez relays this scene in her book *Technology and Critical Literacy in Early Childhood*, co-authored with Carol Branigan Felderman, describing how, over the course of the next several weeks, in class and in her backyard, the children explored several angles. For one, they investigated the messages in the Topsy Turvy video, creating a word cloud to analyze how many times certain words appeared on the product's website compared to the words on a page from a website about gardening. (The words "tomatoes" and "grow" were dominant on the gardening site, with the words "order" and "Topsy Turvy" appearing most often on the product site.) Second, they investigated and documented whether the Topsy Turvy planter would work at all. They planted one group of tomato plants in the ground and another group above the ground using the Topsy Turvy planter. Then they watched, day after day, to see what would grow.

The story of T.J. and the tomato plants shows what can happen when adults listen closely to children's questions and then equip them on their journey to find the answer. It offers a case in point about the interdisciplinary nature of STEM learning in the younger years. And it stands as an example of how information technology, whether YouTube videos or Google search, can be harnessed to empower young children to seek and find answers. Roll all of that together, and you've got an exemplar of how to build foundational skills for becoming media smart and critically literate—able to access and analyze media of all kinds, and savvy enough to start to discern the motivations behind messages and messengers. In a world in which the president of the United States regularly makes claims with no evidence and calls news outlets "fake" as soon as they uncover unflattering information about him, being able to identify and sort out reliable information becomes a survival skill of some urgency.

But here's the catch: the tomato plant activity would never have happened without the guidance of an adult who understood how to use the media to propel children's learning and build critical thinking skills. This was an adult who knew how to keep children's questions about the world at the center of the endeavor without sliding off into trainings on how to click on the right buttons and without fretting that the kids were watching YouTube for more than their allotted minutes.

Adults who know how to teach these skills are the Sacagaweas of the 21st century, guiding the next generation through thickets of information. But where exactly are these adults? And where are the learning settings that enable them to work with children and their families on in-depth projects of this kind? In T.J.'s case, the kindergarten classroom was part of a private school in a relatively well-off section of Washington, DC, where professional parents have time to visit and assist. (I have interviewed Vasquez, who is a professor of education at American University, and heard her speak at national forums; it was a lucky opportunity for T.J. and his classmates to have her assigned to help them for those tomato-planting weeks.) In schools with far fewer resources and much higher ratios of children to adults, you would be hard-pressed to find teachers who have any training in using technology in inquiry-based media literacy and STEM learning projects. In pre-K and childcare settings, it can be even more difficult, given educators' lack of computers and adequate compensation to explore these concepts at all. Families and young children might find a few examples of these projects on display in a public library, but even then, there is little guarantee that librarians have training on how to teach this, let alone know how to apply it for younger kids.

This is why I, and many others, have been arguing that media mentors—whether they be librarians, teachers, or family engagement specialists—must fill this gap. The library world has already started to embrace the possibilities of media mentorship, detailed in the 2016 book *Becoming a Media Mentor: A Guide for Working with Children and Families* (Campbell & Haines). Pioneers in the field of early education, led by the TEC Center at Erikson Institute and others, are helping to build frameworks for skills and training. But as these inspiring efforts take off, we have to make sure that critical thinking skills and the tenets of media literacy—not simply teaching how to use technology or log in to software programs—are front and center.

When Vasquez led her son and his kindergarten peers on their tomato adventure, technology use was not the aim of their project. However, Vasquez was not shy about harnessing tech tools to help kids learn. Not only did the children gain the experience of searching for and finding the video of the commercial for the Topsy Turvy planter on YouTube, but they were encouraged to use the "pause" feature to take their time, to look at pictures and listen to words, to ask questions and look at the images to try to answer them, and to start to grasp the broader messages of the commercial. They even acted out various scenarios and thought up new dialogues for the characters on screen.

Using websites about planting, Vasquez was able to show the children what it looks like to find an authoritative site for gardeners to hone their craft instead of a website aimed at selling a product. She knew how to find and use Tagxedo and Wordle software to generate word clouds and explained to her son that they are designed to show the frequency and emphasis that different website authors put on different words. When Vasquez's son asked why the video didn't show men using the less-strenuous planting method and only showed them using shovels, she knew to use that as an opening for a conversation about gender stereotypes relating to images he could see and understand.

The National Association for Media Literacy Education defines media literacy education as helping "individuals of all ages develop the habits of inquiry and skills of expression that they need to be critical thinkers, effective communicators and active citizens in today's world" (National Association for Media Literacy Education, n.d.). This is not something that teachers are able to simply add to their already-stuffed daily routines without support. They will need guidance, models, and additional professionals in their classrooms, libraries, and coaching programs to expose them to this way of thinking, teaching, and learning. Helping children to develop habits of inquiry, a component of what the Trust for Learning calls ideal learning, requires a teacher to have already developed some of those habits of inquiry herself.

In short, filling our schools with more Vivian Vasquez's will not happen overnight. As an Amazon.com reviewer of one of Vasquez's earlier books (*Negotiating Critical Literacies with Young Children (Language, Culture, and Teaching Series)* wrote in 2016: "I just despair of finding teachers with the skills and commitment to adopt this approach."

Creating this new corps of mentors—which I would argue is a critical piece of protecting democracy in the 21st century—is going to involve a concerted effort to "upskill" today's librarians and educators with training in media literacy education. A 2018 project in Maryland, led by Conni Strittmatter, who at the time was director of youth services at Harford County Public Library, and involving me and my team at New America, provides a key example. The project began as a 12-month effort to create a peer-coaching program for librarians to learn media mentorship, and it resulted in an online tool kit and training workshops that are now being used in at least half a dozen county library systems across the state. It's an exciting endeavor, and yet the more that we talk to librarians about what they want to get out of the program, the more that I realize how media literacy education may be the biggest hurdle to clear. For many, the first topic on their mind is what to tell all the parents who ask how to curtail their children's technology use and who ask about how to set time limits. Those questions are only one part of media mentorship—they are what media literacy expert Faith Rogow calls "media management."

> **"Creating this new corps of mentors—which I would argue is a critical piece of protecting democracy in the 21st century—is going to involve a concerted effort to 'upskill' today's librarians and educators with training in media literacy education."**

The next topic on the mind of many librarians and teachers is how to teach children to use technology skillfully—how to take care of devices and protect passwords, how to download materials and use the keyboard, how to upload and share videos, and how to use various apps. These are what we on the Maryland library project have termed "media mechanics." Children and adults certainly need these skills, but technology devices and formats change so rapidly that it may not be worthwhile to spend exorbitant amounts of time on these skills when children are very young.

Then there is the third "M" that we see as critical to media mentorship: media literacy education. And yet that is the one that gets the least amount of attention among parents, and is, as the Amazon.com reviewer pointed out, not likely to be on the mind of teachers either. Some may argue that kindergartners are too young to think about sources of information and what is *behind* the videos, games, websites, books, and billboards in their everyday lives. But as Vasquez, Rogow, and other pioneers in inquiry-based learning and critical literacy have taught us, there are many age-appropriate methods for helping to build these critical thinking skills in young kids. With ideas and guidance from media mentors, educators and parents can learn to take advantage of children's natural curiosity to build their critical thinking skills about all the messages they see and hear.

For T.J. and his classmates, critical thinking skills grew organically out of the questions they were asking about the world around them. "What started as an inquiry into how to plant tomatoes," Vazquez wrote, "turned into a bigger cross-curricular event," in which young children learned how to deconstruct an everyday text, think about the methods used by different messengers, and take on the role of analyst and investigator (Vasquez & Felderman, 2013).

> **"With ideas and guidance from media mentors, educators and parents can learn to take advantage of children's natural curiosity to build their critical thinking skills about all the messages they see and hear."**

They probably also learned that products do not always work as advertised. The kids did find that tomatoes can grow upside down. But, as Vasquez related in her book, a big rainstorm that year led to another discovery as well: the Topsy Turvy Tomato planter® "absorbed so much water that the entire container fell to the ground, snapping the plant in two" (Vasquez & Felderman, 2013). A better video, her son suggested, would have "talked about what to do when it rains instead of doing all that video on backbreaking work!"(Vasquez & Felderman, 2013).

Lisa's Essentials

1. **Start with children's questions, not with the technology.**
2. **Use technology to slow down instead of speed up** (e.g., take advantage of the pause button).
3. **Model what it looks like to search for information across multiple types of media.**
4. **Seek opportunities to point out the names of creators and developers of multimedia,** just as you might point out an author's name on the cover of a book.
5. **Don't let media management (e.g., time on screen) and media mechanics (how to use the devices and software) overshadow the quest for media literacy.**

References

Campbell, C., & Haines, C. (2016). *Becoming a media mentor: A guide for working with children and families*. Chicago, IL: American Library Association.

National Association for Media Literacy Education. (n.d.). *The core principals of media literacy education*. New York: NAMLE. Retrieved from: https://namle.net/publications/core-principles/.

Vasquez, V. M. Reviewer comment from Amazon.com user Taamier posted on July 17, 2016 on Amazon.com webpage selling *Negotiating critical literacies with young children (language, culture, and teaching series).* Accessed on July 12, 2018. Available at: www.amazon.com/Negotiating-Critical-Literacies-Children-Language/dp/0805840532.

Vasquez, V. M, & Felderman, C. B. (2013). *Technology and critical literacy in early childhood.* New York: Routledge.

Learn More about Lisa's Work

- Lisa Guernsey, *Screen Time: How Electronic Media–From Baby Videos to Educational Software–Affects Your Young Child* (New York: Basic Books, 2012).
- Lisa Guernsey, "In the Age of Fake News, It's Never too Early to Start Teaching Kids Media Literacy," *Slate*, November 8, 2017.
- Lisa Guernsey, "Maryland Libraries Build a Peer-Coaching Program to Train Media Mentors," *EdCentral* blog post published by New America, July 11, 2018 at www.newamerica.org/education-policy/edcentral/maryland-libraries-build-peer-coaching-program-train-media-mentors/
- Lisa Guernsey & Michael H. Levine, *Tap, Click, Read: Growing Readers in the World of Screens* (San Francisco, CA: Jossey-Bass, 2015).
- Lisa Guernsey, "A New Program Has Helped Bring Better Media Literacy to Ukraine," *Slate*, May 9, 2018.

Lisa Recommends

- Vivian Vasquez & Carol Branigan Felderman, *Technology and Critical Literacy in Early Childhood* published in 2013 by Routledge.
- Cen Campbell & Claudia Haines, *Becoming a Media Mentor: A Guide for Working with Children and Families*, published in 2016 by the American Library Association.
- Conni Strittmatter, "Media Mentorship: In Three Parts," blog post published on February 2, 2018 for the Association for Library Services to Children.
- *Peer Coaching Media Mentorship Toolkit*, a free resource designed for librarians and developed through a grant from the Maryland State Library: https://sites.google.com/view/hcpl-media-mentorship-toolkit
- Faith Rogow, Chapter 7, "Media Literacy in Early Childhood Education: Inquiry-Based Technology Integration" in *Technology and Digital Media in the Early Years: Tools for Teaching and Learning*, a book edited by Chip Donohue and published in 2015 by NAEYC and Routledge.
- *Delivering Ideal Learning*, an online resource and guidebook developed by the funder collaborative Trust for Learning. The website includes a statement of principles that focuses on what the authors describe as "a commitment to play, relationship-based interactions, an ecologically-focused, child-centered perspective; equity; and a strength-based and inquiry-based approach with children, adults and families": www.trustforlearning.org/ideal-learning/

Chapter 16

Digesting the iScreen Decade
What Should Media Makers, Policymakers and Philanthropy Do Next?

Michael H. Levine

In 2007, the Joan Ganz Cooney Center launched as a research and field-building organization just as young children – appearing on the fledgling YouTube channel – were taking their first "swipes" on their parents' smartphones. Recall the surprise of watching curious tots moving their fingers across televisions, magazines, and newspapers, expecting an interactive experience to magically transform their parents' analog world. A decade into the iScreen generation, it is difficult to imagine work, social exchange, play, or parenting without the screens and powerful supercomputers to which they are connected.

Back then I wrote that America's children were growing up "in a Jetsonian world" of futuristic, smart digital learning tools, but that the research enterprise to understand the new environment was trailing far behind the technological marvels. I noted, with evident hyperbole, that we knew so little about the impact of digital media on children's learning it was as if we were locked in the Flintstones' era where mobility and communications were governed by foot power and looney birds. Much has been done to inform the scientific and public debate since. Research has focused on ways to bolster quality media content development and to encourage adult–child interactions. Educators and policymakers have embraced new technologies to focus less on consumption itself and more on the potential of digital media to promote deeper learning pathways, adapted to the unique needs of every learner.

> **"A decade into the iScreen generation, it is difficult to imagine work, social exchange, play, or parenting without the screens and powerful supercomputers to which they are connected."**

Yet, despite billions of dollars of investment, a plethora of research studies, and guilt-inducing punditry about the impact of ubiquitous modern media for kids, most parents, and experts, are on the fence about the role technology is playing in advancing or limiting children's learning and healthy development. In an era of fake news, toxic political discourse, and widening socioeconomic divides, what should we take away from a decade marked by both innovation and confusion?

In 2020, the kindergarten students who entered the formal education system at the dawn of the iScreen Decade will graduate from high school. They will certainly have a set of new media skills and experiences unlike any of past generations. But most will also have missed out on the benefits that optimists pointed to just a decade ago. Below, I take stock of the past decade to make some conclusions and to help guide media designers, policymakers, and philanthropies in prioritizing the needed new investments in digital media for young children. Drawing from my perch studying digital media research, design, and practice and helping to lead one of the world's most iconic nonprofit educational media organizations, I submit that we have five key priorities:

1. **Placing children's learning and development front and center**. For eons, communications and media platforms – from books and newspapers to telephones and television – were designed principally for adult use. In the past decade, producers have demonstrated how the interactive screen can open up fonts of knowledge and social experiences for children. Unfortunately, commercial interests have not prioritized the unique capabilities of these new technologies to advance children's social, cognitive, and physical development. Most children are not benefitting from "blended" learning models, across time and space, or immersive experiences that may be possible with the next generation of hardware and software. In fact, one could argue that the lack of compelling learning gains over the past decade, and new stresses in our anytime, anywhere work culture, has brought new attention to the original indictment of television, referred to as the "vast wasteland" by FCC Commission Chairman, Newton Minow in 1961. More than five decades later, we have leapt ahead in the ubiquity of media offerings for young children, but we have not yet provided signposts and milestones to help their parents successfully navigate the "digital Wild West."

2. **Promoting equity and opportunity for deeper learning.** Research at the Cooney Center (Rideout & Katz, 2016) and by other groups indicates that girls, children of color, and children in rural communities are not able to access the same experiences that lead to developing their own "islands of expertise," and mastery of deep and complex learning dispositions that are needed for success in the global economy. More than one in four low-income Latino families and new immigrants are what we refer to as the "underconnected," lacking full and low-cost access to the internet. Low-income, rural, and children of color are also far less likely to gain

access to high-quality digital programs offering complex content in math, science, and engineering.

3. **Encouraging intergenerational co-viewing and deeper peer exchange.** Young children learn more when the adults in their lives are engaged in active "serve and return" interactions. The Center and others have documented best practices among today's diverse families and stimulated a series of designs intended to promote "learning together," in intentional parent–child exchanges which extend "beyond the screen." Professional and policy standards promulgated by the American Academy of Pediatrics, NAEYC, the Fred Rogers Center and the US Departments of Education and Health and Human Services have adopted this research (Academy of Pediatrics, Council on Communications and Media, 2016; Department of Education & US Department of Health and Human Services, 2016; National Association for the Education of Young Children & Fred Rogers Center for Early Learning and Children's Media at Saint Vincent College, 2012). However, life in communities is textured and complicated: in a world where preschoolers consume about three hours of media a day and their parents ten hours, rich social exchange often takes a back seat to modern convenience. Media producers can encourage parents and children to turn off and tune out of their digital lives more regularly. They can also use new insights in early learning and brain development to design for deeper relationships in immersive experiences that encourage family playtime, empathy, and perspective taking.

4. **Helping parents gain the skills needed to navigate the digital Wild West.** In spite of technology's ubiquity in young children's lives we have often lost sight of the critical importance of parents' role in helping their children make intentional and informed choices. Our data have consistently shown that parents have great confidence in the potential of educational media to inform, connect, and inspire children, but that they also seek greater information, skills training, cultural resonance, and practical controls (Rideout, 2014).

5. **Promoting educational standards and industry incentives.** During a time of weakening US educational performance, producers have often shirked their responsibility to produce evidence-based educational products for children and families. A decade ago, the Cooney Center's scan of products labeled educational in the marketplace found that claims of efficacy were misleading, at best. A decade later we have made only scant progress in creating learning standards that can be trusted by parents and educators. There are other worrisome failures of the marketplace, including incursions on privacy and crass advertising techniques by corporations intent on gaining a foothold among an increasingly powerful demographic – children and youth.

So, what can media makers, policymakers, and philanthropy do as we approach the year 2020? Can the potential of modern technologies to deepen early educational experiences ever be realized? Yes, but . . .

First, we need Congress, state leaders, and the private sector to up their games! As a first step toward developing a national commitment for effective digital innovations in education, Congressional leaders and new governors (there will be 36 beginning terms in 2019) should convene digital media and learning summits across the US, to assess existing evidence of successful programs and to map new investments in technologies for children's learning. In preparation for the summits, industry leaders should be challenged to announce their own new R&D initiatives to help stimulate creativity including new design challenges and more deliberate "technology for good" programs. Every policymaker should have a constructive and clear position on the role that technology can – and should not play – in young children's learning.

Second, industry, policymakers, and philanthropy must create new incentives for universal digital participation. Kids' enthusiasm for digital activities presents a great "hook" for teachers and busy parents to diffuse their responsibilities, but if educators and parents themselves do not become technically proficient, the full range of digital possibilities – and the access to new technological tools – will effectively be reserved for the more privileged. Despite billions of dollars invested in infrastructure programs such as E-Rate and expanded community after-school programs, most low-income, rural, and minority children have limited access to the best technology-assisted learning available today. Importantly, they lack appropriate guidance and attention from adults on how best to use and leverage the technology. They can build on innovative models developed by corporations like Intel and Google, nonprofit leaders such as the Boys & Girls Clubs, and Girl Scouts, and the federally supported 21st Century Community Learning Centers. It is time to create a place in every community where young children can confidently gain technology skills. These digital learning hubs should expose children to high-quality, engaging digital tools that integrate language and literacy development with deep content learning.

> **"Kids' enthusiasm for digital activities presents a great 'hook' for teachers and busy parents to manage their responsibilities, but if educators and parents themselves do not become technically proficient, the full range of digital possibilities – and the access to new technological tools – will effectively be reserved for the more privileged."**

Third, the public media system needs new purpose and diverse investors. In 1967, the Carnegie Commission on Educational Television reached the conclusion that a well-financed and well-directed educational television system, must be brought into being if the full needs of the American public are to be served. Five decades later, the system needs to reboot its core educational mission, and get on a path to long-term sustainability. The significant erosion in television ratings in reaching vulnerable families is already of great concern to public broadcasters. Public media, with support from both public and private investors, must greatly expand its R&D function, including a larger commitment to designing mobile and immersive offerings that encourage family engagement. In an era where 300-plus stations are no longer needed to deliver educational media, producers must redouble their outreach programs to successfully engage low-income families, especially recent immigrants. Retooling efforts must also define a usable, personalized framework for parents to make decisions about content for their children, bring new producers from culturally diverse backgrounds into the mix, and produce tangible educational outcomes that are based on research that deeply engages educators themselves. A new Commission to envision an appropriate business model to sustain the system is also timely.

Fourth, educators and parents need full access to community and expert-led rating systems and curation tools, based on scientific research standards and tied to developmental stages. Great resources already exist organized by Common Sense Media and others, but these guidelines must be rolled out in new ways to lower-income and non-English-speaking parents and their children's teachers. These families' concerns should be central to how these recommendations for parent–child interaction are encouraged through new messengers such as faith-based, physician, and library media mentors.

Fifth, let's integrate media use into parent supports and professional practice. Studies of parent involvement in early learning and its influence on school performance indicate that alignment between home and school experiences are critical to later success. However, formal learning environments have not yet adapted to the types of digital media innovation that would support optimal learning and child development. A decade of research shows that young children are exposed to digital media both early and frequently. Surveys also find that over three-quarters of K-5 teachers and almost half of pre-K teachers are using technology with their young charges. These findings suggest that training early educators is both urgently needed and potentially powerful in setting parents and children on a trajectory for confident engagement with digital technologies.

Policymakers and philanthropies should explore new ways to support teacher quality, including an emphasis on digital practices. The first generation of Massive Open Online Courses (MOOCs) did not result in widely available platforms for educators of young children to build their digital-age teaching skills. But notable experimentation is underway from pioneers at Erikson Institute, Khan Academy, University of Washington, and other professional groups. As more early learning professionals explore digital technologies, a new line of pedagogical practices to address the needs of the diverse early learning workforce will be critical. One idea I presented nearly a decade ago is still timely: let's use the social entrepreneurs represented by organizations such as City Year, Teach for America, and Jumpstart to create a *digital teacher corps* whose goal will be to ensure both foundational and digital literacy for all children.

"These findings suggest that training early educators is both urgently needed and potentially powerful in setting parents and children on a trajectory for confident engagement with digital technologies."

Finally, foundations should invest in a national public engagement effort. Research from the FrameWorks Institute indicates that experts have failed to explain the social and economic stakes if every child does not master modern tools and learning methods (FrameWorks Institute, 2018). Digital media use has often been framed in the public debate by the risks of too much consumption, isolation, and the concomitant social and public health consequences. These widely advanced messages create barriers to moving a purposeful learning and child development agenda forward. Important issues ranging from STEM career pipelines – to net neutrality – to overhauling community access programs for low-income and rural families, are policy questions that must be reframed to emphasize the fundamental values of progress and prosperity that we all hold dear.

These priorities imagine the roaring 2020s as the decade when digital media and learning opportunities will be family-centered, universally available, and of enduring impact. Looking back on a decade sometimes characterized as the dawn of the iTot generation, the only confident prediction I can make is that the "next breakthrough" in digital media and learning will be … well, unexpected!

Michael's Essentials

1. **Relationships matter most!** Educators need to step back and consider an issue that is too often overlooked: the depth and quality of their relationships with students. Research on young children's developing brains and self-regulation as active learners shows that having relationships with adults at home and in the community are the most robust predictors of positive attributes in our lives across the lifespan. Most important, intentional "playful learning" should gain higher priority across settings – we need only look at the amazing strength of global brands like Sesame, Lego, and Disney to understand the magic of play in building essential relationships.

2. **Let's scale "blended learning" models that promote learning across settings.** Five decades after *Sesame Street* revolutionized the use of television to educate children at home with vital school-readiness skills, we still need to build a bridge between informal and formal learning. One very promising area that the Cooney Center is researching is the power of digital play to engage students. A recent survey found that the overwhelming majority of teachers using games in schools point to positive benefits of personalized, blended learning (Takeuchi & Vaala, 2014). A new guide from the Center and Asia Society also details the benefits of digital play in establishing the roots of civic participation and global citizenship (Shapiro, 2018).

3. **Reward failure: real innovation starts by taking risks.** Educators have become too hesitant to try something new which might fail because they are so concerned about accountability. We need experimentation with new media platforms to help accelerate change. In a recent series of studies of the digital innovation and family engagement space, the Cooney Center and New America have been mapping and tracking ways in which creative uses of technologies can strengthen early learning while strengthening families (2018).

4. **We need to "rethink the brain."** Beginning in the first year of a baby's life, where synaptic connections are being molded like a sculptor chiseling a block of marble, until they graduate from high school, children are experiencing remarkable leaps and bounds in their capacities. New insights in behavioral neuroscience and in learning and developmental science can help educators gain a richer understanding of early literacy and language development or, for example, the role that digital games can play in helping children focus or to be kind to their peers. Educators should pay close attention to the pioneering language development work of Pat Kuhl, the new focus on "good for you digital games" developed by Adam Gazzaley and Constance Steinkuehler, and the work on digital media use and executive level functioning by neuroscientists Melina Uncapher and Daphne Bavalier. Finally, every preschool and elementary school educator should check out the pioneering community development work using digital media platforms underway by both *Sesame Street* in communities, as well as the Bezos Family Foundation based on the pioneering book by Ellen Galinsky, *Mind in the Making*, and their "brain-building" campaign, Vroom.

References

American Academy of Pediatrics, Council on Communications and Media. (2016). Media and young minds. *Pediatrics*, *138*(5). e20162591. DOI:10.1542/p3ds.2016-2591.

Cooney Center & New America. (2018). *Integrating technology in early* literacy *(InTEL) 2018*. New York: The Joan Ganz Cooney Center at Sesame Workshop; Washington, DC: New America. Available online at www.newamerica.org/in-depth/family-engagement-digital-age/integrating-technology-early-literacy-intel-2018/.

Department of Education & US Department of Health and Human Services. (2016). *Early learning and educational technology policy brief.* Washington, DC: US DOE.

FrameWorks Institute. (2018). *Crossing the boundaries: Mapping the gaps between expert and public understanding of STEM learning environments.* Washington, DC: FrameWorks Institute.

National Association for the Education of Young Children & Fred Rogers Center for Early Learning and Children's Media at Saint Vincent College. (2012). *Technology and interactive media as tools in early childhood programs serving children from birth through age 8*. Washington, DC: NAEYC; Latrobe, PA: Fred Rogers Center for Early Learning and Children's Media at Saint Vincent College.

Rideout, V. J. (2014). *Learning at home: Families' educational media use in America.* A report of the Families and Media Project. New York: The Joan Ganz Cooney Center at Sesame Workshop.

Rideout, V. J., & Katz, V. S. (2016). *Opportunity for all? Technology and learning in lower-income families.* A report of the Families and Media Project. New York: The Joan Ganz Cooney Center at Sesame Workshop.

Shapiro, J. (2018). *Digital play for global citizens*. New York: The Joan Ganz Cooney Center at Sesame Workshop.

Takeuchi, L. M., & Vaala, S. (2014). *Level up learning: A national survey on teaching with digital games.* New York: The Joan Ganz Cooney Center at Sesame Workshop.

Learn More about Michael's Work

Barron, B., Cayton-Hodges, G., Bofferding, L., Copple, C., Darling-Hammond, L., & Levine, M. H. (2011). *Take a giant step: A blueprint for teaching children in a digital age.* New York: The Joan Ganz Cooney Center at Sesame Workshop.

Guernsey, L., & Levine, M. H. (2015). *Tap, click, read: Growing readers in a world of screens.* San Francisco, CA: Jossey Bass.

Takeuchi, L., & Levine, M. H. (2013). Learning in a digital age: Towards a new ecology of human development. In A. Jordan & D. Romer (Eds.), *Media and the well-being of children and adolescents.* New York: Oxford University Press.

Michael Recommends

- Parenting for a Digital Future: http://blogs.lse.ac.uk/parenting4digital future/. This blog, led by contributing author Professor Sonia Livingstone of the London School of Economics, offers keen insights on global trends in digital learning research and public policy.
- DML Connected Learning Research Network: https://clrn.dmlhub. net/. This interdisciplinary research network, led by Dr. Mimi Ito, is dedicated to understanding the opportunities and risks for learning

afforded by today's changing media ecology, as well as building new learning environments that support effective learning and educational equity.

- New America's Education Policy: www.newamerica.org/education-policy/. The site synthesizes original research and policy analysis to help solve the nation's critical education problems, crafting objective analyses, and suggesting new ideas for policymakers, educators, and the public at large.

- Joan Ganz Cooney Center: http://joanganzcooneycenter.org/. The Joan Ganz Cooney Center conducts independent research and features innovative policy and industry perspectives on the challenges and opportunities of educating children in a rapidly changing media landscape.

- *The new co-viewing: Designing for learning through joint media engagement.* Takeuchi & Stevens. (2011). New York: The Joan Ganz Cooney Center at Sesame Workshop. www.joanganzcooneycenter.org/publication/the-new-coviewing-designing-for-learning-through-joint-media-engagement

- American Academy of Pediatrics, *Media and Young Minds: Council on Communications and Media, Policy Statement,* October 2016. http://pediatrics.aappublications.org/content/early/2016/10/19/peds.2016-2591

Chapter 17

Childhood 2040
A Wish List

Warren Buckleitner

Before I predict how technology might influence the next generation, let me make a confession. This isn't my first attempt. Eighteen years ago, I wrote an essay called "A Day in the Life of a Kid in the Year 2020." (The original essay was published in the January/February 2000 issue of *Children's Technology Review* – author's own publication – updated in 2012 and now in 2019 https://childrenstech.com/blog/archives/8494). I took the topic personally, because my two daughters were then four- and eight-years-of-age, and technology was changing quickly.

Today both daughters are in their twenties, and one has just given birth to her first child. This gives me another personal reason to look back at my original forecast, and forward to the year 2040 for my grandchild.

So, what did I get right last time? Twenty years ago, I was correct that our gadgets today would be thinner and faster; and that I'd be thicker and slower. I focused mostly on the hardware, however. I incorrectly assumed that once Moore's Law had connected all our cheap, powerful devices, that a lot of our problems would be solved. I never thought that the biggest challenge today would be dealing with too many apps, videos and more, and understanding how they are used to support developmentally appropriate practice.

We Are Living in Amazing Times

Before I look into my crystal ball, let me zoom way out for some larger context. We're all part of a very special generation – the first to whisper to the electronic genies who know the answer to any question and can play any symphony. They go by names like *Siri, Alexa* or *Hey Google* and they embody how far microprocessor-related technologies have evolved in the past 20 years. In fact, of all of the previous 7,500 or so generations of Homo sapiens, it is ours that is the lucky one that gets to see this magic happen. So, if nothing else, you'll always have the best "when I was a kid" stories when we're old codgers. As children, we may have seen the dawn of Computer-Aided Instruction (CAI) systems. Starting in the 1960s, microprocessor fever

Photo 17.1 Jenna and Sarah Buckleitner at the computer
Photo credit to Warren Buckleitner

started capturing the imaginations of a few innovators including CAI pioneer Patrick Suppes, who predicted in 1966, "In a few more years millions of schoolchildren will have access to what Philip of Macedon's son Alexander enjoyed as a royal prerogative: the personal services of a tutor as well informed and as responsive as Aristotle" (Suppes, 1966). Suppes and others kept dreaming, testing and making products to tease the imagination. As CAI continued to evolve into the '70s, Alan Kay sketched his theoretical $500 Dynabook giving us a preview of today's iPad and Chromebook (both cost about $500).

As Seymour Papert was writing his book *Mindstorms* (1980) about the importance of letting children learn to code, I was an early childhood consultant at the High/Scope Foundation, where I found an article describing how electronic learning settings could create a "golden age" for education, where technology-enhanced learning could affordably deliver a high-quality individualized education (Banet, 1979). The early '80s and '90s were heady times when desktop and laptop computers were introduced, and the first home video game consoles replaced the huge arcade behemoths.

Photo 17.2 Sarah Buckleitner
Photo credit to Warren Buckleitner

An especially noteworthy moment was at 10:14 am Pacific Time, on March 12, 2010, when Apple's Steve Jobs demonstrated the first iPad. It wasn't even designed for children, but it would change everything for them. Parents started posting baby videos of children happily dabbing at iPads, as the mouse and keyboard became obsolete. Software became apps and many people thought hardware had reached the evolutionary finish line. I recall when software pioneer and co-founder of The Learning Company, Ann H. McCormick, called the iPad "the computer we always dreamed of." Almost overnight the children's app market went from a few hundred titles to tens of thousands. The golden age seemed within reach.

It's Nearly 2020. Was I Right?

I'm thrilled that my daughter now has a car with integrated phone/GPS and lane detection features, and that she can contact me by text, instant message or video chat before her morning commute. My daughter's pediatrician has much better tools than we had as young parents, for things like accurate ultrasounds. Mobile technology has made us the first generation of parents to be physically far from our grown children, but we have the capacity to be psychologically closer. As a software reviewer, things have never been better on the one hand, or more confusing on the other. Among the tens of thousands of children's apps are some beautiful examples of developmentally appropriate practice with apps that support active inquiry. Our recent installation of a VR system in our library has been highly successful, and tablets rarely break.

> **"Mobile technology has made us the first generation of parents to be physically far from our grown children, but we have the capacity to be psychologically closer."**

Pies in the Face

Fred Rogers said "I got into television because I saw people throwing pies at each other's faces and that, to me, was such demeaning behavior. And if there's anything that bothers me, it's one person demeaning another. That really makes me mad" (Hollingsworth, 2005, p. 11). I suspect that Fred Rogers would be very mad about the new forms of hidden digital pie throwing that's going on in the app stores. A child with a mobile device and a password can fall into a web of manipulative videos and apps that might contain inappropriate content or simply steal valuable playtime. The worst, which I review every week, tease young children with age-appropriate themes, but lead to some form of sponsored content that eventually demand payment to play. These types of activities are especially deplorable, because they're specifically engineered for profit.

In schools, too many early childhood settings are using powerful technologies, but they deliver un-powerful curriculum. There's little thought to app selection, and elementary level teachers are still heavily influenced by behavioral benchmarks. And sadly, we still live in a time when the academic value of a child is measured by a single Saturday morning encounter with a three-hour paper and pencil SAT test. Despite having the tools, we're not using them as well as we could to support the development of young children. So, despite our vast leaps on the hardware front, we're still far from Banet's golden age of learning.

> **"In schools, too many early childhood settings are using powerful technologies, but they deliver un-powerful curriculum."**

It's Nearly 2020. What Should We Be Doing by 2040?

The quality of my grandchild's digital life is in our collective hands – the "us" being the current parents, teachers, librarians, app sellers and designers. Here are some of my essentials:

Warren's Essentials

1. **We must be inspired by the uncompromising standards of Fred Rogers.** We need to apply those old standards to the new media. Thankfully we have a good road map in the form of the 2012 NAEYC/Fred Rogers Center joint position statement (NAEYC and Fred Rogers Center, 2012). It reminds us that while hardware and software will change, the principles of child development remain constant.

2. **Young children must be treated ethically in the digital age.** A good start comes from Europe. Designing for Children's Rights Association (2018), a UNICEF-related group, created a set of guidelines for publishers, called the *Designing for Children's Guide*. These can advise those without a background in child development on issues related to information collection and use of commercial content.

3. **People who run app stores and video delivery services need a reminder that they are delivering products to a rare and special audience – children.** Today, these people include Amazon's Jeff Bezos, Google's Larry Page and Serge Brin, Netflix's Reed Hastings and Apple's Tim Cook. They must understand that children are using their associated markets and make them age appropriate. A good start would be to use a labeling system that children can understand.

4. **Make it easier for the adults who know the children to purchase apps.** Active learning is alive in the app stores, but it's been diluted by millions of free and low-quality apps. That's why it is important for teachers and librarians to have control over the devices in their classroom, so they can swap out an app as easily as a new set of markers or blocks.

5. **Watch children and trust your instincts.** There's good and bad in any technology, so be on the lookout for the good.

6. **Become a media mentor.** Early childhood educators and others who work on behalf of children and families must become vocal advocates (aka media mentors) for quality, pressuring app sellers to "do unto the children of others as you would do to your own children and grandchildren."

7. **Tap into the power technology offers.** As Barbara Chamberlin notes in one of her recent talks (Chamberlin, 2018), we're living in a time when just about any activity can be tracked, from the number of steps you take in a day to the amount you use your vacuum cleaner. This can be creepy, but it can also be used for formative assessment so that busy teachers can make better pedagogical choices. Early childhood educators must have a voice in the debate about data collection.

8. **Make sure every child has access.** Increasingly, those without access to digital device and WiFi are left in the shadows of the information age. Our public libraries and schools must rise to this challenge.

"While hardware and software will change, the principles of child development remain constant."

My Hope for My Grandchild

Alan Kay reminds us that "the best way to way to predict the future is to invent it" (Kay, 1990), and Fred Rogers said, "no matter what the machine may be, it was people who thought it up and made it, and it's people who make it work." (Rogers, 1994, p. 64). A few things are fairly certain about how technology might improve the world for my grandchild. We can assume that the field outside of education will continue to evolve, which could make the future more safe, creative and fun. As delivery drones buzz overhead, fleets of hybrid/electric school buses will shuttle children to schools synced to an individualized learning plan. If a car can park itself, certainly a math curriculum can adapt to a learner. Because every child will be surrounded by a cloud of algorithms, this information can be used to better inform teachers and celebrate development. Better screening and assessment programs will capture medical and psychological problems early and will help insure that no child is overlooked.

The tools for this already exist or will soon be invented. These technologies can fulfill B. F. Skinner's (1961) vision for the teaching machine, and YouTube certainly comes very close to the prediction by Patrick Suppes (1966) of, "the personal services of a tutor as well informed and as responsive as Aristotle." I hope that most schools do actually reach the golden age of education, when John Dewey's ideals for project-based collaborative learning come true and more time can be spent on aesthetics.

To say we're living in exiting times is an understatement. Moore's Law has now reached terminal velocity, and the computers I wanted for my own children in 2000 are now in backpacks. We're the lucky ones because, like any previous generation, we have access to powerful tools that have untapped potential to "make goodness attractive" (per Fred Rogers, 2003), for all children. It's not an easy job, but it's certainly worth it. After all, what grandparent wouldn't want the best for his or her grandchild?

References

Banet, B. (1979). Hands on! Computers and early learning. *The High/Scope Report Number Four*, pp. 33–41, online at https://files.eric.ed.gov/fulltext/ED176856.pdf.

Buckleitner, W. A. (2000). A day in the life of a kid in the year 2 020. *Children's Technology Review*. January/February 2000, online at http://childrenstech.com/2020.

Chamberlin, B. (2018). Shifting the conversation: Important discussions about children and technology. (Dust or Magic AppCamp) on YouTube, online at https://youtu.be/tAuRqktPgB0.

Designing for Children's Rights Association. (2018). *Designing for children's guide*, online at https://childrensdesignguide.org/.

Hollingsworth, A. (2005). *The simple faith of Mister Rogers*. Brentwood, TN: Integrity Publishers.

Kay, A. C. (1990). The best way to predict the future is to invent it. Keynote presentation, *Annual Conference of the Association for Supervision and Curriculum Development*, San Francisco, CA.

Kay, A. C. Rare NHK footage of the Dynabook, online at https://youtu.be/r36NNGzNvjo.

National Association for the Education of Young Children &Fred Rogers Center for Early Learning and Children's Media at Saint Vincent College. (2012). *Technology and interactive media as tools in early childhood programs serving children from birth through age 8*. Washington, DC: National Association for the Education of Young Children and Latrobe, PA: Fred Rogers Center for Early Learning and Children's Media at Saint Vincent College, online at www.naeyc.org/sites/default/files/globally-shared/downloads/PDFs/resources/topics/PS_technology_WEB.pdf.

Papert, S. (1980). *Mindstorms: Computers, children, and powerful ideas*. New York, NY: Basic Books.

Rogers, F. (1994). *You are special: Words of wisdom from America's most beloved neighbor*. New York, NY: Penguin Books.

Rogers, F. (2003). How do we make goodness attractive? *Federal Communications Law Journal*, 55(3), Article 23. www.repository.law.indiana.edu/fclj/vol55/iss3/23.

Skinner B. F. (1961). Teaching machines. *Scientific American*, *205*(5), pp. 90–107.

Suppes, P. (1966). The uses of computers in education. *Scientific American*, *215*(3), pp. 206–220.

Learn More about Warren's Work

Buckleitner, W. A. (2000). A day in the life of a kid in the year 2020. *Children's Technology Review*, January/February 2000, online at http://childrenstech.com/2020

Buckleitner, W. A. (2010). Is the iPad a child's best friend? Why Apple may have created the ultimate plaything for kids. *The New York Times*, online at http://gadgetwise.blogs.nytimes.com/2010/01/30/is-the-ipad-a-kids-best-friend/

CTREX (Children's Technology Review Exchange), online at www.ctrex.us

Warren Recommends

Here are some of my favorite books, articles, blogs, websites, videos.

- *Won't You Be My Neighbor*. If you haven't seen it, this documentary film is essential viewing for anyone who works with children: http://focusfeatures.com/wont-you-be-my-neighbor/
- *On Minor Miracles* by Sarah Buckleitner, the mother of my grandson. Here's a poignant reflection on the wonder and anxiety of human life: https://featherythoughts.com/2018/06/25/on-minor-miracles/
- *Shifting the Conversation: Important Discussions about Children and Technology* with Barbara Chamberlin. If you don't know Barbara Chamberlin,

watch this video. She reminds us that in the future even your vacuum cleaner will collect data. This doesn't have to be bad thing: https://youtu.be/tAuRqktPgB0

- The UNICEF *Designing for Children's Guide* is the start of a much-needed conversation among children's content creators that assumes that we must all take care of children: https://childrensdesignguide.org/principles/

- *OK Go*. Why give children access to technology? The band known as OK Go has its roots in a music camp, when two 11-year-old children decided to start a band. Today, their work merges music with math and all forms of digital technologies. Watch how they use printers, at: https://youtu.be/LgmxMuW6Fsc or visit the OK Go resources for educators at https://okgosandbox.org

Afterword
PastForward: Why We Need Thought Leaders and Media Mentors

Chip Donohue

This book of essays has been a PastForward experience as the contributing authors have looked back and reflected on their work and the evolving state of our understanding about young children and technology. They also shared innovative approaches, recommended next steps and articulated their vision for childhoods in the digital age.

Taking a PastForward perspective is about connecting the dots between what has been, what is and what we imagine could and should be. Each of the authors framed their work around the evidence base from almost 50 years of children's television research and the emerging research about how young children are accessing and using devices that were not designed for them but are ubiquitous in their world – smartphones, tablets, smart speakers, wearables and more. The context in which they all work includes public concerns about health, sedentary behavior, sleep disruptions, problematic screen use, inappropriate content, commercial messages, persuasive design and the rights of children in the digital age. Connecting the dots between what we know is beneficial screen time and the concerns about harmful screen time addresses the dynamic tension between what we know and what we still need to learn. What we all agree about is that it is not as simple as either/or.

I'm taking my PastForward moment now to reflect on issues addressed, lessons learned and next steps described by the thought leaders in their essays. Here are a few of my takeaways from the powerful ideas for your consideration.

Connecting the Dots

In his essay, **Lewis Bernstein** described the need to carry the lessons learned from *Sesame Street* forward into the digital age and identified the shared responsibility of children's media developers, designers, content experts, platforms and educators to produce products that are grounded in child development and draw on the evidence base from more than 40 years of research on what works in children's television. He noted that the digital devices and social media platforms of today are already in children's hands, and that means it is up to us to keep the children safe.

David Kleeman reflected on his career in children's media and reminded us that even as things change, much remains the same. For example, old child development theory can inform the design and use of new digital media. He offered evidence that the past is moving forward by pointing out that while the devices are new, children still: demonstrate familiar play patterns; play with toys; have a love for storytelling and creating; continue to watch television the most despite the proliferation of new screens; schedule their technology and media use.

Ellen Wartella, who has done much of the research we all point to from the age of children's television to the digital age, looked back at the controversies over children's use of the media and technology tools of the day, and brought these concerns forward to the present-day challenges and opportunities digital media offers and how it influences young children, families, educators and developers. She raised the possibility that research may show benefits for children and concluded with advice about the need for more research to answer questions about the impact and implications of digital media use by young children.

Lydia Plowman challenged us to think about what happens when technology disappears. She shared her definition of "ambient computing" and reminded us that for all their tech savvy, young children still need the guidance of a more capable other. She described a distinction between face-to-face (i.e. proximal) support and ways of supporting interaction that are more remote in terms of time and space (i.e. distal). The concepts of "active presence" and "remote presence" were considered and connections with the proximal and distal dimensions of guided interaction were described. And, she discussed the importance of knowing when to step back as the right thing to do and explore ways of providing support that don't depend on face-to-face presence or spoken language.

In "Seeing Is Believing," **Kevin A. Clark** addressed issues of diversity in children's media and discussed the impact on children and society at large. He noted that media, including books, television, films, video games, etc., shapes children's understanding of the world around them and helps them make sense of the people, places and events in their lives. He called on media creators to produce media that includes authentic and varied voices to avoid the "creator–consumer divide" and strongly recommended that people of color play a more vital and influential role in creating, developing and distributing content in their own image and voice to counteract frequent exposure to negative representations.

Sonia Livingstone challenged us to think about children's rights. She shared specific challenges related to legal interpretation, policy implementation and effective enforcement. She identified key issues and essential questions for claiming and protecting the rights of the child, and righting real and potential wrongs as young children navigate the digital age. She concluded with two questions that drive the research and scholarship on children's rights in the digital age. First, how can children's voices be better heard? And, how can children's rights in the digital environment be better addressed?

Shuli Gilutz took up the issue of children's rights from the perspective of designing products for children using child-centered design principles that incorporate children's perspectives, needs and rights, at the heart of the design process. She reminded us that designers must be keenly aware of the physical, cognitive, social and emotional development of the children they are designing for. Her essay concluded with the ten principles of the *Designing for Children's Guide* developed as part of the designing for children's rights initiative with UNICEF.

Susan Edwards introduced us to the concept of digital play in early childhood education and described how digital technology can be effectively integrated into early childhood settings. She pointed out that young children are growing up within digital contexts that require adults involved in their education and care to have knowledge or a perspective on how they understand and think about "digital" in relation to children's lives, as well as to play as a valued pedagogy. She offered us a new conceptual pathway for thinking about what "digital play" is in contexts where young children today are growing up with and using networked digital technologies daily.

In her essay, **Marina Umaschi Bers** identified the benefits of introducing coding in early childhood and made the case for coding being a language that compliments the emphasis on language and literacy in the early years. She argued that coding should not be folded into the disciplinary cluster of STEM and offered an alternative pedagogical approach, "Coding as Another Language." She also introduced programming environments designed for early childhood education such as the ScratchJr app and the KIBO robotic system that teach coding with a literacy approach.

Natalia Kucirkova argued that strong technology design and pedagogy are two necessary sides of the educational coin and explained the context for personalized education and personalized books. She identified benefits of personalized education including giving children choices, motivating them to learn, fostering their curiosity and igniting their wonder and enjoyment of learning. Her focus was on how personalized books provide an example of technology use in schools that focuses on agency and reciprocity. She concluded that interactions that empower children and honor their agency are those that follow her "5As" of personalization: authorship, autonomy, authenticity, aesthetics and attachment.

Jackie Marsh described her work with the "MakEY" (Makerspaces in the Early Years: Enhancing Digital Literacy and Creativity) project that involves seven European countries, and works with partners from across the world. In her essay she considered the value of providing young children with opportunities to tinker, make and hack using a range of tools, including digital fabrication tools and other technologies. She shared key principles that should underpin the work, including: encouraging multimodal, technology-mediated playful learning; fostering maker mind-sets and agentic exploration; valuing both processes and products; and facilitating interdisciplinary work.

Pediatrician **Jenny Radesky** addressed how mobile devices and persuasive design affordances of media interact with parent–child interaction dynamics, using an infant mental health framework. She identified that child characteristics (temperament, regulatory abilities) and parent characteristics (mental health, parenting style) interact in a transactional manner over time to influence child developmental outcomes. She explored the research on how smartphones and tablet computers associate with parent–child interaction and how these affordances affect parent self-efficacy, self-awareness about one's relationship with devices, sense of guilt or polarization about rapidly evolving technology and relevant intervention or digital literacy approaches.

M. Elena Lopez explored the intersection of effective family engagement practices with new digital devices and new ways of communicating with parents and caregivers. She shared examples of technology-mediated and -enhanced practices to illustrate the variety of ways technology is being mobilized to improve communication, increase participation, empower parents and engage families. She also shared examples of family engagement initiatives in formal and informal settings that bring children and grown-ups together to demonstrate the benefits for children and for adults when they engage with each other in a shared experience.

Lisa Guernsey, a leading voice in the media mentor movement, identified the most needed mentorship of all: how to help families, children and educators develop the critical thinking skills that can help to discern quality media from questionable media and successfully navigate the sea of online information that is streaming towards them. She described recent work in helping to develop a new peer-coaching model to support media mentors in Maryland public libraries. She also highlighted ideas and innovations related to media literacy coming from today's children and youth services' librarians.

Michael H. Levine embodied the PastForward idea in his reflections on the iScreen Decade by connecting the progress that has been made and the work that remains to be done to understand the implications for children's media developers, parents and families, educators, researchers, policymakers and philanthropists. He identified priorities, including: a focus on children's learning and development; addressing equity issues; offering opportunities for deeper learning; encouraging intergenerational co-viewing; enabling peer-to-peer learning; enhancing the digital knowledge and skills of parents; and advocating for educational standards and incentives for children's media developers. He offered strategies for putting these priorities into practice and ended with a call to policymakers and philanthropists to support children's media developers, researchers and educators to benefit young children, parents, caregivers and families.

The last essay, by **Warren Buckleitner**, is also a prime example of a Past-Forward perspective. Before he offered his Childhood 2040 Wishlist, he looked back at where we've been and how far technology has come over the past 20 years. He noted examples of developmentally appropriate apps and technology experiences and developers who are returning to old child development theory to guide their design process. He also raised concerns about negative impacts and inappropriate, unethical and manipulative practices aimed at children that "steal valuable playtime." He evoked the spirit of Fred Rogers to remind us that Fred used the media of his day, broadcast television, as a tool for good.

Why Children Need You to Be the Thought Leaders and Media Mentors

In my work around young children and technology with early childhood educators, I have learned that while educators recognize they play the role of digital age decisionmakers and know they are not unequipped for the responsibility of selecting, using, integrating and evaluating technology and children's media, they often feel ill-equipped and underprepared to help young children, parents and families safely navigate the digital age. As many authors shared in their essays, we need to empower early childhood educators to take on the roles of media mentor and emerging thought leader by focusing first on what they do know, not on what they still have to learn about technology, and connect the dots to the lessons learned, provocations and nudges delivered in this collection of essays.

What early childhood educators do know about and have experience with:

- child development theory and principles of early learning;
- developmentally appropriate practice;
- a focus on social emotional learning and the whole child;
- relationships and opportunities for joint engagement;
- evidence-based practices for teaching and learning;
- family engagement strategies that empower parents, caregivers and families.

Here are some next step "essentials" for educators shared by the authors:

- Connect research to practice and adopt evidence-based approaches.
- Become familiar with position statements, principles and guidelines of international early childhood and child health organizations.
- Investigate emerging guidelines for media developers and consider the implications for children and how to support parents and families.
- Learn more about how children use technology in classrooms, beyond the classroom in informal settings and at home.

- Understand the need for children to create media and have access to makerspaces.
- Seek opportunities for ongoing professional development and connected learning.
- Build a local ecology of early childhood technology and media environments, practices and champions that includes: formal and informal educators, teacher educators, researchers, pediatric health professionals, media developers, policymakers, philanthropists and the parents/caregivers who all have a stake in raising young children today.
- Make a commitment to protecting and advancing children's rights.

If we want these tools, and the time children spend using them, to support healthy child development, early learning and early literacy, then we also need to reflect on and confront the powerful influence the grown-ups in young children's lives have as media role models and mentors – for better or worse. We each need to be aware of our own media behavior and habits and then help avoid "parenting without presence" and instead emphasize parenting that is tuned-in, attentive and present.

Did We Pass the Seymour Test?

Marina Umaschi Bers, who studied with Seymour Papert at MIT, wrote a highly recommended article called, "The Seymour test: Powerful ideas in early childhood education" (Bers, 2017), about the importance of having, sharing and learning from powerful ideas. I began this book with that idea and nudged readers to find the powerful ideas within the perspectives and approaches of the thought leaders who wrote the essays.

I am confident that individually and collectively, the authors and this book would pass the Seymour test. There have been many powerful ideas exchanged, numerous provocations offered and even a few gentle nudges about the need for articulating your own powerful ideas beyond these pages to move us all forward. As you reflect on what you've read and learned, consider what powerful ideas you will integrate into your own practice and what you will share with colleagues to improve childhoods in the digital age. What will you do to become an influential and impactful media mentor and thought leader for the young children, parents, caregivers and families you work with?

And as Seymour Papert reminds us, sometimes the most powerful ideas come from the children if we just look, listen and engage with them. His provocation for all who care for, educate and advocate for young children was, "I am convinced that the best learning takes place when the learner takes charge" (Papert, 1993, p. 25).

And his nudge to each of us was, "Rather than pushing children to think like adults, we might do better to remember that they are great learners and to try harder to be more like them" (Papert, 1993, p. 155).

This book contains the words, powerful ideas and innovative approaches of thought leaders from the United States, the UK and Australia. Take what you can from each of them to deepen your knowledge and enhance your practice, and always remember to follow the real leaders – the young children right in front of you. How well we use these powerful new tools rests in very small hands.

References

Bers, M. U. (2017). The Seymour test: Powerful ideas in early childhood education. *International Journal of Child–Computer Interaction, 14,* 10–14. doi.org/10.1016/j.ijcci.2017.06.004.

Papert, S. (1993). *The children's machine: Rethinking school in the age of the computer.* New York, NY: Basic Books.

Learn More

A curated collection of organizations, programs, projects, websites and recent reports to encourage you to dive deeper into key issues, evolving perspectives and innovative approaches to young children and technology.

- **American Academy of Pediatrics (AAP)** *Media and Young Minds:* Council on Communications and Media, Policy Statement (2016) http://pediatrics.aappublications.org/content/early/2016/10/19/peds.2016-2591
- **American Academy of Pediatrics (AAP)** *The Power of Play: A Pediatric Role in Enhancing Development in Young Children* http://pediatrics.aappublications.org/content/142/3/e20182058
- **Amazon** www.amazon.com/
- **American Psychological Association (APA)** *Digital Guidelines: Promoting Healthy Technology Use for Children* (2018) www.apa.org/helpcenter/digital-guidelines.aspx
- **American Psychological Association (APA)** *Treating the Misuse of Digital Devices* (2018) www.apa.org/monitor/2018/11/cover-misuse-digital.aspx
- **Apple** www.apple.com
- **Association of Library Services to Children (ALSC)** www.ala.org/alsc/
- **Australian Department of Health** *Australia's Physical Activity and Sedentary Behaviour Guidelines* (2017) www.health.gov.au/internet/main/publishing.nsf/content/health-pubhlth-strateg-phys-act-guidelines
- **Center for Childhood Creativity at the Bay Area Discovery Museum** *The Roots of STEM Success: Changing Early Learning Experiences to Build Lifelong Thinking Skills* (2018) https://centerforchildhoodcreativity.org/roots-stem-success/
- **Center for Digital Media Innovation and Diversity** https://cdmid.gmu.edu
- **Center on Media and Child Health (CMCH)** https://cmch.tv

- **Center on Media and Child Health Clinician Toolkit** http://cmch.tv/clinicians/
- **Center on Media and Human Development (CMHD)** https://cmhd.northwestern.edu
- **Child–Computer Interaction Group** www.chici.org
- **Children and Technology Research Group** www.de.ed.ac.uk/children-technology
- **Children's Technology Review** www.childrenstech.com
- **Code.org** https://code.org
- **Common Sense Media (CSM)** *Media Use by Kids Age Zero to Eight* (2017) www.commonsensemedia.org/research/the-common-sense-census-media-use-by-kids-age-zero-to-eight-2017
- **CTREX** https://reviews.childrenstech.com/ctr/home.php
- **Designing for Children's Guide** https://childrensdesignguide.org
- **Designing for Children's Rights Association** http://designingforchildrensrights.org/
- **Developmental Technologies Research Group (DevTech)** http://sites.tufts.edu/devtech/
- **Digital Literacy and Multimodal Practices of Young Children (DigiLitEY)** http://digilitey.eu
- **Dubit** www.dubitlimited.com/
- **Dust or Magic** www.dustormagic.com
- **Early Childhood Australia (ECA)** *Statement on Young Children and Digital Technologies* (2018) www.earlychildhoodaustralia.org.au/wp-content/uploads/2018/10/Digital-policy-statement.pdf
- **Early Childhood Futures** www.acu.edu.au/research/our-research-institutes/institute-for-learning-sciences-and-teacher-education/our-research/early-childhood-futures
- **Early Childhood STEM Working Group** *Early STEM Matters: Providing High-Quality STEM Experiences for All Young Learners* (2017) http://ecstem.uchicago.edu
- **Early Learning Lab** *NextGen Technology: Insights and Recommendations to Support the Parents of Children Ages 0–3* (2018) https://earlylearninglab.org/nextgentechreport/#webinar
- **Education Development Center (EDC)** www.edc.org
- **EDC and SRI Education** *What Parents Talk About When They Talk About Learning: A National Survey About Young Children and Science* (2018) www.edc.org/sites/default/files/uploads/EDC_SRI_What_Parents_Talk_About.pdf
- **edutopia** www.edutopia.org
- **EU Kids Online** www2.lse.ac.uk/media@lse/research/EUKidsOnline/Home.aspx
- **FrameWorks Institute** *Early STEM Learning* (2016) www.frameworksinstitute.org/stem-learning.html#early

- **Fred Rogers Center for Early Learning and Children's Media** www.fredrogerscenter.org
- **Fred Rogers Center & TEC Center** *Technology and Interactive Media for Young Children: A Whole Child Approach Connecting the Vision of Fred Rogers with Research and Practice* (2017) www.fredrogerscenter.org/tech nology- interactive-media-young-children/
- **George Lucas Educational Foundation (GLEF)** www.edutopia. org/about
- **Global Family Research Project (GFRP)** https://globalfrp.org/
- **Global Kids Online** www.globalkidsonline.net/
- **Google** www.google.com
- **GoPro** https://gopro.com
- **Institute for Learning Sciences and Teacher Education (ILSTE)** https://lsia.acu.edu.au/about/
- **Institute of Medicine/National Academy of Science** *Transforming the Workforce: A Unifying Foundation* (2015) www.iom.edu/Activities/ Children/BirthToEight.aspx
- **International Communications Association** www.icahdq.org
- **International Society for Technology in Education (ISTE)** *Standards for Educators* (2017) www.iste.org/standards/standards/for-educators
- **Joan Ganz Cooney Center at Sesame Workshop** http://joanganz cooneycenter.org
- **Joan Ganz Cooney Center at Sesame Workshop & New America**

  - *STEM Starts Early: Grounding Science, Technology, Engineering, and Math Education in Early Childhood* (2017) http://joanganzcooney center.org/publication/stem-starts-early/
  - *How to Bring Early Learning and Family Engagement Into the Digital Age* (2017) www.joanganzcooneycenter.org/wp-content/ uploads/2017/04/digital_age.pdf
  - *Integrating Technology in Early Literacy (InTEL)* (2018) www.newa merica.org/in-depth/family-engagement-digital-age/integrating-technology-early-literacy-intel-2018/

- **KIBO** KinderLab Robotics http://kinderlabrobotics.com
- **LEGO Foundation** *Centre for Creativity, Play, and Learning* www.lego foundation.com/en/what-we-do/research-centre/
- **Lifelong Kindergarten Group at the MIT Media Lab** www. media.mit.edu/groups/lifelong-kindergarten/overview/
- **London School of Economics (LSE)** www.lse.ac.uk
- **Lucas Education Research (LER)** www.edutopia.org/about
- **Makerspaces in the Early Years: Enhancing Digital Literacy and Creativity (MakEY)** http://makeyproject.eu

- **Mediatech Foundation** www.mediatech.org
- **Minecraft** https://minecraft.net/en-us/
- **MIT Media Lab** www.media.mit.edu
- **Moomins** www.moomin.com/en/
- **National Association for the Education of Young Children (NAEYC)** *Technology Resources* www.naeyc.org/resources/topics/technology-and-media
- **National Association for the Education of Young Children and the Fred Rogers Center** *A Joint Position Statement on Technology and Interactive Media as Tools in Early Childhood Programs Serving Children from Birth through Age 8* www.naeyc.org/resources/topics/technology-and-media
- **National Association for Media Literacy Education (NAMLE)** http://namle.net/
- **New America** www.newamerica.org
- **UN Office of the High Commissioner for Human Rights (OHCHR)** *UN Convention on the Rights of the Child* www.ohchr.org/en/professionalinterest/pages/crc.aspx
- **Our Story** https://itunes.apple.com/us/app/our-story-for-ipad/id681769838
- **Parenting for a Digital Future** http://blogs.lse.ac.uk/parenting4digitalfuture/
- **Personalised Stories** www.ucl.ac.uk/ioe/departments-and-centres/departments/learning-and-leadership/personalised-stories
- **Preparing for a Digital Future** http://blogs.lse.ac.uk/parenting4digitalfuture/
- **Radesky Lab** https://sites.google.com/umich.edu/radeskylab/home
- **Ready4K** https://ready4k.parentpowered.com
- **Royal College of Paediatrics and Child Health (RCPCH)** *The Health Impacts of Screen Time: A Guide for Clinicians and Parents* (2019) www.rcpch.ac.uk/resources/health-impacts-screen-time-guide-clinicians-parents
- **ScratchJr** www.scratchjr.org
- **Seesaw** https://web.seesaw.me
- **Sesame Workshop** www.sesameworkshop.org
- **Silicon Valley Community Foundation** *Lost Connections in a World of Connectivity* (2018) www.siliconvalleycf.org/sites/default/files/publications/cel-tech-report-2017.pdf.
- **SRI International** www.sri.com
- **Tagxedo** www.tagxedo.com
- **Technology in Early Childhood Center at Erikson Institute (TEC Center)** http://teccenter.erikson.edu
- **Text4baby** www.text4baby.org
- **Toca Boca** https://tocaboca.com

- **Toy Association** *Decoding STEM/STEAM: The Toy Association Strategic Leadership Committee Report* www.toyassociation.org/ App_Themes/toyassociation_resp/downloads/research/whitepapers/ decoding-stem-steam.pdf
- **Trust for Learning** *Delivering Ideal Learning* www.trustforlearning. org/ideal-learning/
- **United Nations International Children's Emergency Fund (UNICEF)**

  - *Convention on the Rights of the Child* (2017) www.unicef.org/crc/
  - *The State of the World's Children 2017: Children in a Digital World* www.unicef.org/publications/files/SOWC_2017_ENG_WEB. pdf

- **US Department of Education & Department of Health and Human Services** *Guiding Principles for Use of Technology with Early Learners* (2016) https://tech.ed.gov/earlylearning/principles/
- **WGBH** www.wgbh.org
- **W.K. Kellogg Foundation (WKKF)** www.wkkf.org
- **Wordle** www.wordle.net
- **YouTube** www.youtube.com/
- **Zero to Three** *Screen Sense: What the Research Says About the Impact of Media on Children Under 3 Years Old* www.zerotothree.org/resources/ series/screen-sense

Index

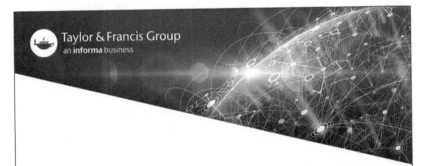